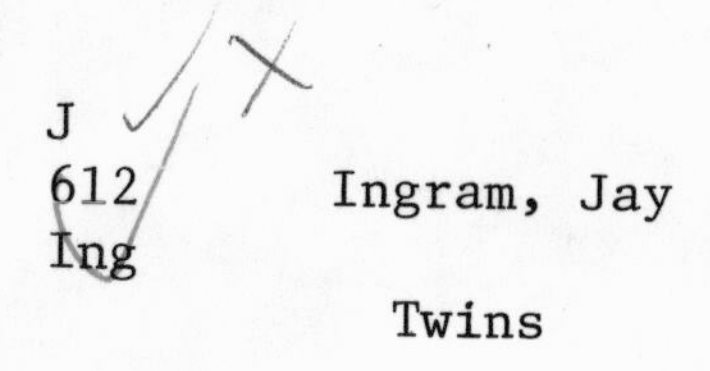

WASHINGTON COUNTY PUBLIC LIBRARY
3 1991 00119587 7

Jay Ingram
Illustrations by Harvey Chan

Simon and Schuster Books for Young Readers
Published by Simon & Schuster Inc., New York

Originally published in Canada by Greey de Pencier
Books, Toronto.
Published by Simon and Schuster Books for Young Readers
A Division of Simon & Schuster Inc.
Simon & Schuster Building
Rockefeller Center
1230 Avenue of the Americas
New York, NY 10020

Designed by Wycliffe Smith
Printed and bound in Canada

10 9 8 7 6 5 4 3 2 1

Library of Congress Cataloging-in-Publication Data

Ingram, Jay.
Amazing investigations. Twins.

Includes index.
Summary: Examines the subject of human and
animal twins, scientific studies of twins, and
unusual stories about twins.
1. Twins—Psychology—Juvenile literature.
2. Twins—Juvenile literature. [1. Twins]
I. Title.
BF723.T9I54 1989 612'.6 87-32366

ISBN 0-671-66263-5

Contents

Famous Twins

Who are the most famous twins in the world? That's a tough question. There are the Puntous sisters of Quebec, Sylviane and Patricia, who compete in the triathlon – swimming, cycling and running – and usually end up hitting the finish line at about the same time. Jean and Auguste Picard were great French balloonists who lived about a hundred years ago. The identical twin Pekinel sisters play classical music on twin pianos. There are even twin American skiers, Phil and Steve Mahre.

But none of these twins are super-famous. If they aren't the most famous twins in the world, who are? You decide – here are some of the candidates.

CHAPTER ONE

KATE AND DUPLICATE

Two American advice columnists, Dear Ann (Landers) and Dear Abby (van Buren), are identical twin sisters, born Pauline Esther and Esther Pauline Friedman. When they were children, they dressed alike, slept in the same bed and double dated. Their schoolmates teasingly called them Kate and Duplicate. In fact, Ann and Abby were never separated until the day they were married – in a double ceremony, of course. For years, however, they have written their columns for rival newspapers, and each has millions of loyal readers all over North America.

CHAPTER ONE

POTO AND CABENGO

"Cabengo padem manibadu peetu."

"Doan nee bada tengkmatt."

"Poto, pinit."

"Pinit?"

"Yah."

This was a conversation between two American twin girls named Grace and Ginny Kennedy. A few years ago the Kennedy twins made headlines as the twins who had made up their own language. That's why you couldn't understand that conversation. They made up the words, and only they could understand them.

Their secret language was discovered by chance. The twins' parents were concerned that the girls weren't speaking English very much, even when they were nearly 7 years old. In fact, they weren't going to school, because the Kennedys felt that Ginny and Grace couldn't communicate with other kids.

Their parents knew that the two girls chattered a lot to each other in their room, but they just assumed it was baby talk. Only when experts started to work with the girls did it become clear that they were speaking their own language. They called each

other Poto and Cabengo. (Both names appear in the conversation.)

It was clear right away that their language wasn't English with a strange pronunciation, or German. (It might have been German because their grandmother spoke German to them when they were little.) It wasn't even a mixture of German and English. Had they invented a completely new language?

Experts spent months carefully studying tapes of the twins talking to each other, and finally they came up with the answer. Grace and Virginia, or Poto and Cabengo, were speaking mostly English, but they changed it in curious ways. They would replace some of the letters in a word, so an *f* might become a *p*, or a *sh* a *t*. The word "pinit," for instance, means "finish." The twins wouldn't always change words the same way, however, so an outsider never really knew how to translate their speech.

Since the Kennedy twins were "discovered" in the late 1970s, they've gone on to learn English and go to school just like other kids their age. But for a while these twins were speaking a secret language that nobody else in the world could understand.

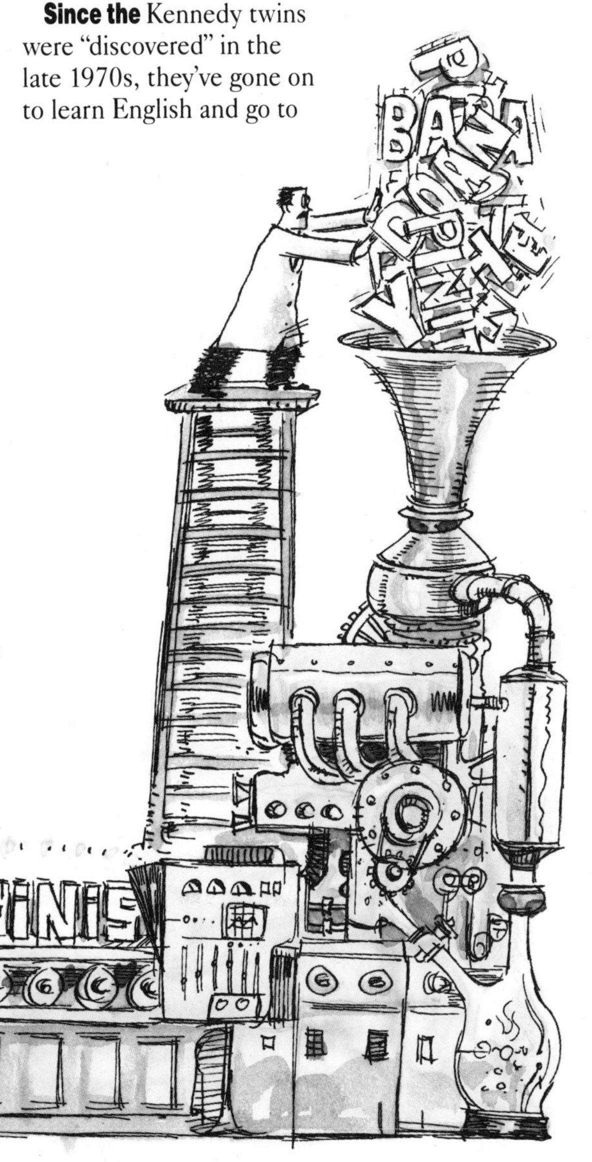

SUPERSTARS

Step outside on a starry night in early spring and you can see the oldest pair of twins in existence. To most people who see them today, they're just another couple of stars in the sky. But if you'd lived in ancient Rome, or Greece, or 2,000 years before that in Babylonia, you would have known these stars as "the Twins." Just think, as you stand and look at them, that a Babylonian kid might have done the same thing, more than 4,000 years ago. Today we call these stars Gemini, the Latin word for twins. But who were they before they became stars?

In the ancient world, sailors swore by Gemini for their safety. In fact, the expression "by Jiminy" started out as "by Gemini." They knew the twin sons of the god Zeus, Castor and Pollux, had sailed with the legendary Jason and his ship the *Argo.* Jason and his daring crew had

C H A P T E R   O N E

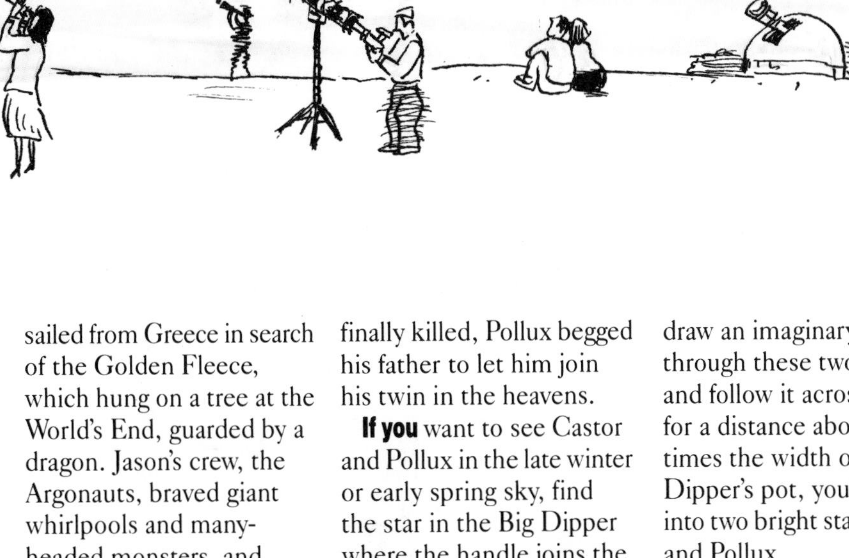

sailed from Greece in search of the Golden Fleece, which hung on a tree at the World's End, guarded by a dragon. Jason's crew, the Argonauts, braved giant whirlpools and many-headed monsters, and Castor and Pollux saved them during a tremendous storm. When Castor was finally killed, Pollux begged his father to let him join his twin in the heavens.

If you want to see Castor and Pollux in the late winter or early spring sky, find the star in the Big Dipper where the handle joins the dipper. Then find the star on the other side of the dipper at the bottom. If you draw an imaginary line through these two stars and follow it across the sky for a distance about five times the width of the Big Dipper's pot, you'll run into two bright stars: Castor and Pollux.

CLOSE BROTHERS

Chang and Eng were two twins born in Thailand in 1811. As young men they moved to America and joined the circus, eventually settling down in North Carolina. There they decided to use Bunker as their last name. They married sisters, Sarah and Adelaide, and had a total of 22 children: Chang and Adelaide had 10, and Eng and Sarah had 12!

Now that is a lot of children, but so far there's nothing particularly outstanding about the story of these twins that would make them famous, is there? Well, what if you knew that in 1811 the country of Thailand was called Siam – would that make a difference? That's right: Chang and Eng were the original Siamese twins.

They spent their whole lives joined together at the side, by a band of tissue that ran from the bottom of their ribs down to about the level of the navel – in fact, they had only one navel between them. (It turned out after they died that their livers were connected too.) But they led as normal a life as possible. They actually had separate homes in North Carolina, and they would spend three days in one, then three days in the other.

On January 12, 1874, Chang caught bronchitis, and his health failed rapidly. He died in his sleep that Friday night. When Eng realized Saturday morning that his twin was dead, he is reported to have said, "Then I am going too." He died two hours later.

Today there are more than 1,000 descendants of Chang and Eng. None of them are Siamese twins.

A ROMAN LEGEND

There's no doubt that if we were living in the Roman empire over 2,000 years ago, the most famous twins of all would have been Romulus and Remus. There were statues of them, they appeared on coins, and everybody knew who they were: the founders of the city of Rome.

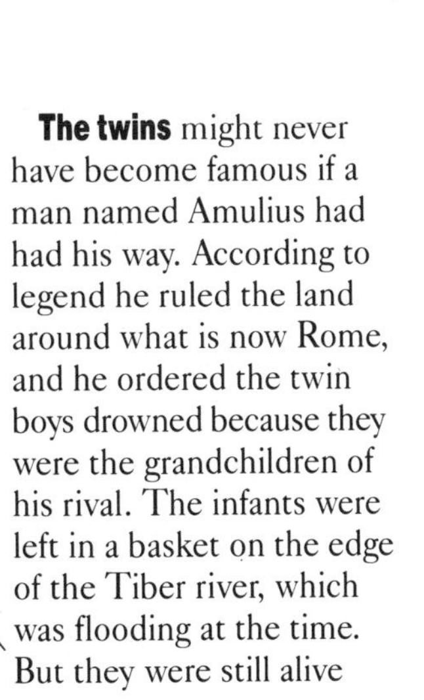

The twins might never have become famous if a man named Amulius had had his way. According to legend he ruled the land around what is now Rome, and he ordered the twin boys drowned because they were the grandchildren of his rival. The infants were left in a basket on the edge of the Tiber river, which was flooding at the time. But they were still alive when the waters went down, and a female wolf found them. She nursed the two boys, keeping them alive until they were found by the king's herdsman. He took them home, and he and his wife raised the two boys. Their real identity was eventually discovered, and although Remus was killed, Romulus went on to found Rome, one of the greatest cities of the world.

SPACE TWINS

How can one twin get older than the other? There's a pair of twins who play an important role in one of the most famous scientific theories of all time: Einstein's Theory of Relativity. Part of that theory is called the "twin paradox."

Two twins live on Earth in the future. One of them is an astronaut who travels regularly to the stars in state-of-the-art spaceships. These future ships travel at nearly 90 percent of the speed of light. That would be about 269,000 km (167,000 miles) every second, much faster than any spaceship we've built yet. When the astronaut twin takes off and gets up to top speed, an unexpected thing happens. Einstein's theory predicts that time would move more slowly for the twin in space than for the twin at home; at that speed, time would move *twice* as slowly. So for every minute the twin in space spends eating or exercising or writing home, *two* minutes pass on Earth.

Although this idea has been around since 1905, and jet planes with incredibly precise atomic clocks on them have proven that time *does* slow down if you're

moving fast, it's still a very difficult thing to imagine. But as far as scientists can tell, it's true: if you can travel near the speed of light, time slows down for you.

Slowing down time is just one of the weird things that happen if you can move nearly as fast as light. You'd also start to shrink, and your weight would start to grow. But the time problem is the most amazing. It means that when the space-traveling twin returns home after 10 years (for him), his formerly identical twin and all their friends would have aged 20 years. To make the twins the same age again, you'd have to send the Earth-bound twin out to space for 10 years of high-speed travel. But then when he returned, all their friends would be 10 years older than both of them – all because the twins had been traveling at close to the speed of light.

What do you think the next pair of famous twins will be famous for? A pitcher and catcher on a baseball team? A pilot and a copilot? A beautiful ballerina and her dancing partner? Maybe. But the next famous twins will probably do what twins do all the time: the unexpected.

Exactly the Same But Different Too

Dawn and Shaune Shannon never expected this! It's true that their husbands, Ronnie and Donnie Shaw, proposed to them on the same day, then married them on the same day. The two couples honeymooned in the same place. They even lived on the same street in Dallas, Texas. But all these coincidences didn't prepare them for this: here they were at the South Arlington Medical Center, the same day, the same time, both having a baby!

An amazing set of events, but the kind of things that seem to happen often to certain people – twins. Besides looking alike and sometimes acting alike, twins may have the same experiences at the same time. In this case, Ronnie and Donnie are twins, and so are Dawn and Shaune.

CHAPTER TWO

The twins that are most like each other are called identical twins. There are good reasons why they are alike in so many ways. Identical twins actually start life as one single egg inside their mother's womb.

CHAPTER TWO

An egg that's going to develop into a baby starts to divide as soon as it's fertilized by the father's sperm. The one-celled egg splits in half to become two cells, which stay stuck to each other. Then those two split again to become a cluster of four cells, and so on and so on. Once it's divided up like this, the egg is called an embryo. Finally, nine months later, that one egg cell has developed into a baby made up of billions and billions of cells.

But an egg that turns into identical twins does something unusual right at the beginning. It produces an embryo that splits in two. The two halves are no longer attached to each other, and each one goes on to make its own baby. But because these two cell clusters originally came from one egg cell, the babies they make are exact copies of each other. They're identical twins.

You might think that because the egg splits in half, identical twins should be only half the size of other kids. But the egg splits when it is still so small that you can't see it without a microscope. There's lots of time left for the two twins-to-be to grow a little faster and catch up.

Twins are usually just a little smaller than other children when they're born. Each weighs about 2.6 kg (a little under 6 lbs.) as opposed to 3.35 kg (a shade over 7 lbs.) for the average single baby. There's just not as much room inside the womb for two babies as there is for one. When the two together reach about the same size as one *big* baby – about 5 kg (11 lbs.) – they're ready to be born. Usually they arrive a few weeks earlier than single babies.

Identical twins are pretty rare – one pair is born for about every 300 births. Even so, there could be as many as 30 million pairs of identical twins around the world! Scientists aren't really sure why identical twins happen. They know the developing egg splits in two just as it starts growing, but they don't know what causes the split.

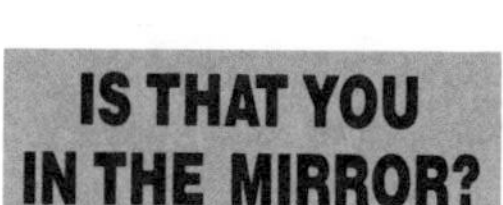

IS THAT YOU IN THE MIRROR?

Sometimes you can tell whether identical twins have split early or late. Twins that split early in the womb look almost exactly the same: their hair is the same color, their teeth look the same, they're often the same height and weight.

But other identical twins are alike in a different way. They're called "mirror image" twins, because one looks like the mirror image of the other. You know that if you look in the mirror, your image is reversed: if you have a dimple on the right side of your mouth, the face in the mirror has a dimple on the left side. The same is true of mirror-image identical twins. If one has hair that swirls from left to right, the other's will swirl from right to left. One might have the same fingerprint patterns on her right hand that her twin has on her left hand. Sometimes when these twins are tiny babies, they even do things in mirror-image ways! One baby will lie in his crib curled up to the right, and the other will curl up to the left.

Scientists think mirror-image twins develop that way because the cluster of cells splits in half just a little later than usual. When it does finally split, even though it's still very tiny, it already has a right side and a left side. One twin develops from what would have been the left side, and the other from the right side. That's why one twin might end up with a tooth that sticks out on the right, while the other's sticks out on the left. There are even cases where one twin has the internal organs on the usual side of the body, but the other twin has them reversed: the heart on the right, and the liver on the left.

If the little embryo develops even further before splitting, the babies may be Siamese twins. These are twins that didn't split completely in the womb – they're still joined together when they're born. Sometimes they're not held together by much more than some skin, and doctors can separate them without any trouble. But often Siamese twins are very difficult to separate because they share some crucial organs, like the liver or even part of the brain. Then separating them endangers their lives.

Until modern times it was usually too risky to separate Siamese twins. Today surgeons are able to do very delicate operations, and they can separate many Siamese twin babies. But there are still some who might die if separated, and they live their whole lives joined together.

DO YOU WEAR YOUR GENES TO SCHOOL?

Scientists say identical twins look alike because they have identical sets of genes. If you've inherited your father's nose or your mother's smile, what you've really inherited is some genes; his nose genes or her smile genes. You can't see genes; they're much too small. But they're coiled up in every cell of your body.

Genes control all the chemical processes that go on invisibly in your body. Most of the time you aren't aware of them, but some, like the genes for sex, hair color or eye color, have effects that everyone can see. There are also genes that control your fingerprint patterns, the shape of your face, whether you'll go bald when you get older, and about 100,000 other things too.

Identical twins have exactly identical sets of genes. That's why they're the same sex. And they're the only people on Earth with those gene sets.
If you're not an identical twin, your closest gene companions are your brothers and sisters: even though they might look a lot like you, only about half your genes are the same as theirs. You share a quarter of your gene set with your grandparents, and only an eighth with your first cousins. That's why your cousins usually don't look at all like you. But identical twins share *all* their genes.

EXACTLY THE SAME BUT DIFFERENT TOO

Even so, identical twins do not look absolutely, perfectly identical. You've probably found that once you get to know a pair of twins very well, you can usually tell them apart. There's always something that gives them away: one might have a slightly crooked smile, while the other might have freckles in different places. But how can identical twins be different, if they both come from the same egg and have the exact same genes? The differences that develop in twins prove that although your genes control your sex and some of your looks and thousands of other things about you, they're not the whole story of who you are.

What else can there be? All your experiences – the food you eat, the people you know, the good times and the sad times you have – can leave their mark on you just as your genes do. Strangely enough, this may happen even in the womb. Sometimes one identical twin is bigger than the other at birth. When that happens, doctors guess that one twin somehow got a bigger share of nourishment in the womb, and so got a head start on the other. Another experience that may make a difference is that one twin has to be born first; the second is left to struggle to be born for a few more minutes. (The record for the longest delay before the second birth is 147 days!)

Scientists and doctors aren't sure of all the things that happen in the womb, but they do know that the result is that these "identical" babies turn out to be slightly different. Even their fingerprints are not exactly the same, although they're very close.

TWINS THAT DON'T LOOK IT

Identical twins are only half the twin story. There are also fraternal twins, and they're completely different. They are twins because both are in their mother's womb at the same time, and they are usually born within minutes of each other. But they don't come from one egg that splits in two, as identical twins do.

Fraternal twins develop from two different eggs, and the two embryos develop separately from each other. They are just like two brothers, or two sisters, or a brother and a sister who happen to be born at the same time. (In fact, the word "fraternal" comes from the Latin word *frater*, meaning brother.) They may not even look very much like each other, just as some other brothers and sisters look as though they belong to different families.

Fraternals are different from identical twins in other ways too. There are more of them: in North America there are about twice as many pairs of fraternal twins as there are pairs of identicals. It's easier for mothers to produce two embryos from two eggs at the same time than to produce one egg that splits into two.

What's really curious, though, is that fraternal

CHAPTER TWO

THE YAM CONNECTION

twins are born more often in some countries than in others. Identical twins are born at about the same rate everywhere in the world: at the equator or near the poles, in rich countries or poor, one pair of identical twins is born for about every 300 births. But fraternal twins can be as common as one pair for every 22 births, which was once the rate among the Yoruba tribe in Nigeria, or as rare as only once in 160 births in Japan.

The story of the Yoruba tribe in Nigeria is a perfect example of just how mysterious twins still are. When scientists first studied the Yoruba people in the late 1960s twins were appearing once every 20 births or so. But today that very high twin birthrate has slowed dramatically, to about one pair for every 42 births. What's happened?

The secret might be food. Yoruba women used to eat a lot of yams (also called sweet potatoes). The Nigerian version of these vegetables contains chemicals that cause more than one egg to be released at once from the mother's ovaries. When that happens, it's a lot easier to have two eggs fertilized and have fraternal twins. But over the last few years, the Yoruba's diet has changed; they're now eating fewer yams and more rice, milk, sugar and bread. Could fewer yams mean fewer twins? The yam theory is only a guess, but wouldn't it be interesting if sweet potatoes on the plate meant twins in the crib?

It's not just geography that has an effect on the birth of fraternal twins. Some mothers are more likely than others to have twins. The older a mother, and the more children she already has, the more likely she is to have fraternal twins. And if she already has one set of twins, her chances of having another set are increased. In 1961, Mrs. M.L. Pearson of Jacksonville, Florida, had her seventh set of twins. Other mothers have had six sets.

Even the mother's family – or the father's – may have something to do with it. Twins seem to run in families. Scientists aren't totally convinced that people inherit the tendency to have twins from their parents, but they say it's possible. How else do you explain a story like this from 1861? You might need a computer to follow it:

Twin brothers got married. The first brother and his wife had five pairs of twins. Seven of these ten children got married, and four of them had twins as their first children. The other brother (remember him?) and his wife had eleven children, including four pairs of twins. Now that's what you call running in a family!

The wonderful thing about twins is that there are a lot of pieces to the puzzle, like the mother's age, or the twins in her family or her husband's family, or even what she's eating. But scientists aren't sure how to put the pieces together and finish the puzzle. Even today, they have to admit that they really don't know why some mothers have twins.

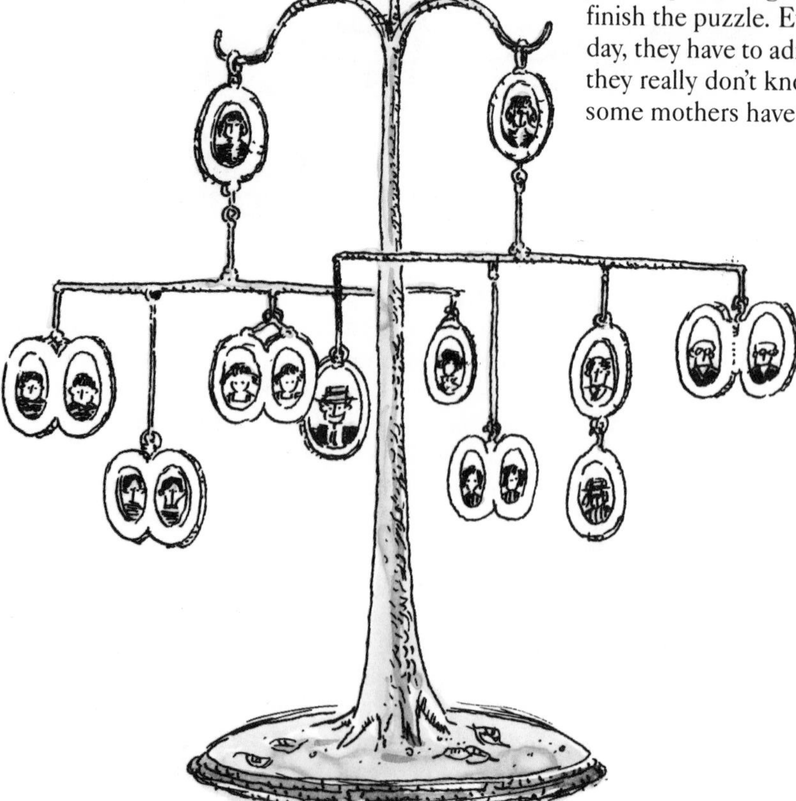

THE TWIN THAT VANISHED

The newest mystery of all is the vanishing twin. Imagine this: some scientists say that as many as seven out of every ten of us began our lives as twins. But in most cases the other twin has vanished! The twin that survives never knows that he or she was, for a short time, a twin. The disappearance occurs early, around the fourth month in the womb.

These vanishing twins have just been discovered, because scientists can now use sound waves to make a picture of the inside of the womb very early in a woman's pregnancy. At that time the pictures often show the faint signs of what might be two embryos. Yet, five months later, the women give birth to single babies. No trace of the twin. What happened? The scientists can only guess that the missing twin embryos stopped developing when they were only a few months old. Why? It's just like everything else about twins: no one is really sure!

Animal Twins

ometimes the simplest questions are the hardest to answer. (Questions like "Why can't we start dinner with dessert?" for instance.) It's the same thing with twins. One really simple question is "Why are there so few human twins?" Another is "Why are there any human twins at all?" Oddly enough, they're both *tough questions to answer. But in the animal world, the questions are completely different.*

CHAPTER THREE

One thing's for sure: in the rest of nature twins are pretty boring. Two babies at a time? Toads can lay 30,000 eggs at a time. If a pair of houseflies started breeding in April, and all their young survived and bred too, they would have 191,010,000,000,000,000,000 descendants by August. Even dogs and cats would think human twins are a yawner: they have five or six kittens or puppies at a time. We who have only one baby most of the time are definitely in the minority, but we can brag about the fascinating company we keep: chimpanzees, gorillas, elephants, condors, whales, dolphins, horses and vampire bats all have only one baby at a time.

It's strange: why doesn't every animal or fish or bird have the same number of babies?

In nature the important thing is not just to give birth to as many offspring as possible. It's for as many offspring as possible to *survive.* Sometimes that's not easy. We lead very safe lives, compared with animals like the sea turtle. When a baby sea turtle hatches, he has to climb out of the hole in the sand where his egg was laid, then run as fast as he can across the beach to the safety of the ocean. Sometimes this little turtle, no bigger than the palm of your hand, has to run the width of a football field before he hits the water, with hawks and gulls just waiting on the beach for an easy meal.

CHAPTER THREE

BIG AND LITTLE

It's pretty risky for frogs and fish too, because most of them just lay their eggs in the water and hope for the best. Sometimes the eggs hatch before they're

discovered by animals with a taste for eggs, and sometimes they don't.

So one reason some animals lay hundreds or even thousands of eggs is that only a few of them survive. And usually the smaller the animal, the more babies they produce, because small animals and their eggs are easy to eat. Another factor in survival is the amount of time the parents are going to spend bringing up the children.

Some fish actually hide their newly hatched babies inside their mouths to protect them from danger. Water bugs sometimes glue their eggs to the father's back, and he floats near the surface of the water to keep the eggs aerated, so they hatch sooner. But most insects, frogs and fish don't spend any time at all with their babies. They just lay their eggs and leave them to fend for themselves. Since that's pretty risky, these animals try to increase their offspring's chances by laying lots of eggs, so that a few will survive.

But for bigger animals who have less to fear, one baby may be just the right number. The mother can be pretty sure her baby will live, because she protects it all the time. And that takes so much of her time and energy that six or seven babies would be just too much. One is enough.

So for every animal there is an ideal number of babies, whether it's one or a dozen or 50 or 10,000.

COTTON-TOPS AND WHOOPERS

Chimpanzees and gorillas almost always have one baby at a time. So do most monkeys, but the cotton-top tamarin, a tiny monkey that lives in Colombia, is an exception. The mother cotton-top always has twins, but it's definitely not easy for her. Her two twins weigh a quarter as much as she does when they're born. That would be like a human mother giving birth to two 7-kg (15-lb.) babies – four times the normal weight of a single baby! No wonder the cotton-top mother keeps her older daughters around to help.

CHAPTER THREE

One of the rarest and most spectacular North American birds has twins just about every time it has babies. It's the whooping crane, the huge white bird that builds its nest in Wood Buffalo National Park in northern Canada.

Strangely, whooping cranes don't do very well at raising their twins. The two babies compete for the available food, and there's usually only one winner. That means only one survivor. The whooping crane population has grown from fewer than 20 birds in the whole world 40 years ago to well over 100 today. But there are still too few whoopers to allow that second egg to be wasted. Scientists decided they could use it to help the whooping cranes survive.

Every spring they raid the whoopers' nests and take out one of the two eggs. Then they fly from the nesting site in the Northwest Territories all the way south to Idaho, carefully keeping the eggs warm all the way. In Idaho the scientists slip each whooping crane egg into the nest of one of its closest relatives, the sandhill crane, when the sandhill crane isn't looking. The sandhill mother and father then hatch that egg and raise the little whooper as their own. An adopted twin!

Scientists hope that there will soon be two separate flocks of whooping cranes: the main one that nests in the Northwest Territories and winters in Texas, and another that travels with the sandhill cranes, moving between Idaho and New Mexico. Then even if disaster strikes one flock, the other should be able to survive.

THE ARMOR-PLATED QUADRUPLET-MAKER

Most animals have more than one baby at a time. Almost all these animal twins and triplets and quadruplets and so on are fraternals. There are very few identical babies born in the wild. There is one animal, though, that has identical babies, but they're not twins. They're quadruplets!

The animal is the nine-banded armadillo, a little armor-plated creature that lives in South and Central America. It is spreading fast through the southern United States too. Armadillos root around in the soil and under dead leaves looking for the insects, spiders, snakes, earthworms and termites they eat.

The armadillo has a complete bag of escape tricks. When chased by a coyote or dog, it will dig itself right into the earth with its sharp claws. It can be completely underground in about two minutes, even in ground so hard you'd need a pick to break it up. If the predator gets there before the armadillo has finished digging its hole and grabs the tail that's sticking out, the arma-

dillo just digs the edges of its shell into the earth and won't let go. And if there isn't even time to start to dig, it'll roll up in a ball, so that all you can see is what looks like an armor-plated grapefruit. It can even walk on the bottom of shallow ponds and streams, and there are stories of armadillos gulping down air until they can just float away from danger.

They sound indestructible, but these days the armadillos' biggest enemy is one for which they have no defense: the automobile. When an armadillo is startled by a car, it often makes the fatal mistake of jumping straight up in the air, and the car hits it. They'd do much better just crouching under the car as it drives over them, but that's not what armadillos are programmed to do.

They're pretty unusual animals, aren't they? But we're just getting to the best part: when a nine-banded armadillo gives birth, she produces four identical quadruplets, every time.

Lots of animals have four babies at a time without going to the trouble of having identical quadruplets. How do the armadillos do it? The egg that turns into four baby armadillos stops dividing, doing nothing for weeks, at a time when most egg cells would be dividing rapidly and turning into embryos. But the armadillo egg just waits and waits. When it finally does start dividing again, it quickly produces four separate embryos.

The long wait must have something to do with the special results: the quadruplets. But it doesn't explain *why* these animals always have identical quadruplets. At a time when many wild animals are becoming rarer, armadillos are expanding their territory every year. Are they surviving better because they are born in four identical copies? Like so many mysterious questions about twins, this one has no answer yet.

But armadillos have given us a better idea of what being "identical" really means. Baby armadillos are identical because they're all from the same

egg, and they have the same genes. But each quadruplet is different in important ways: some are bigger than others; some have hearts or kidneys or livers that are different sizes; and most of them have very different levels of various body chemicals. So they're not perfectly identical.

Why not? When human twins are different weights at birth, it's always been assumed that one was better nourished than the other. But that wouldn't totally explain the many dramatic differences between armadillo quadruplets. Some scientists think that when the original egg is divided up into four, it's not a totally equal division. They think each armadillo baby ends up with a different-sized piece of the egg, so it gets a different amount of the egg's microscopic machinery. It's like cutting up a cherry pie – some kids get more cherries than others. That might explain why the "identical" armadillos aren't really identical.

CHAPTER THREE

SIMPLE QUESTIONS?

Now that we've finished this quick mini-tour to see how many babies animals have, let's come back to those two simple questions: "Why do we humans have so few twins?" and "Why do we have twins at all?"

Most scientists think humans usually have one baby because that's the best number for us. Twin babies are born smaller and earlier than usual, so they're not as strong and healthy as most single babies. That means they have a tougher time getting safely through the first few weeks of life. In fact, when doctors and their treatments weren't as sophisticated as they are today, life was so difficult for newborn twins that many of them died. Until recently there were no children's hospitals to care for underweight and early babies. And giving birth to twins was much more difficult for the mother too.

Some twin experts have an idea that back when many people were nomadic, even a successful twin birth might have spelled trouble. If you're on the move constantly, trying to get enough to eat, never stopping in one place for very long, carrying two babies and feeding them can be very difficult. They think that may be why some nomadic peoples used to go to the terrible extreme of killing one twin or both, even if they were born healthy.

Research on modern parents, especially mothers, shows that they aren't able to give each of their twins as much time and attention as they would give a single child. In fact, they often treat the twins as if they were one child: for instance, putting both to bed at the same time even if only one is tired.

So it seems that human beings probably settled into having just one child at a time because having more than one was a little risky, both for the two babies and for their mother. Like most mammals, we have ended up having the number of babies we can care for properly.

That may make sense, but you then have to wonder why humans have twins at all. That's the second "simple" question. Even today twins can be in danger if they are born too small or too early. The risk is much smaller now. But if there is *any* risk to having twins, why didn't we just stop having them altogether? This is a real mystery.

Whatever answer you come up with, you've got to be able to put all the pieces of the puzzle together: why older mothers have twins more often, why mothers who already have children are more likely to have twins, and why even food (remember the Yoruba?) seems to affect whether you're likely to have twins. Scientists are really at a loss to answer this question. You just have to think of twins as an accident – a happy accident!

Supertwins

In May 1984, two horses named Question and Answer were born in Colorado. That doesn't sound too strange, does it? Well, they were born at about the same time, but that's not too odd either. And they were identical twins. Now that's interesting, because horses don't have twins very often. But what makes Question and Answer really fascinating is that they were born from different mothers!

CHAPTER FOUR

How could they be identical twins and yet have different mothers? This time the horses had some help from scientists. It all started with just one fertilized egg that started to develop into a colt in one mare. The scientists removed that tiny horse embryo when it was only a few dozen cells and put it into a dish in the lab. Then they brought in the micromanipulator, a kind of microscope with hands and tools attached to it like a robot. While the micromanipulator held the tiny horse-to-be very gently, a blade sliced it in half.

Slicing this early embryo in half did absolutely no harm to it. It just created two little bunches of cells. The researchers then put one little cell cluster in the womb of one mare, and the second cluster in another mare. Neither of these mares was the original mother. Eleven months later, both gave birth: one had Question, the other had Answer. Because the two colts came from the same original egg, they're identical twins.

It's a dramatic development, and horse breeders think there will be many opportunities to use it. If they have a mare that produces good colts, they'd like that mare to have lots of babies. But eleven months is a long time to wait between colts. So a colt embryo is taken from that mare almost as soon as she's pregnant, and it's split and put into two other mares. Then one colt has become two, and the special mare can get pregnant again right away. British scientists have done the same sort of thing with pigs, cattle and sheep.

CHAPTER FOUR

AMAZING EMBRYOS

This tricky twinning also shows something pretty amazing about early embryos, embryos that are only 50 or 100 cells. They're tough! Not only can they survive being split in half with a blade, but each half can go on to produce a complete animal. That's probably what happens when identical human twins are created naturally from one egg. But these early animal embryos go even further: they can even be cut into quarters, and each quarter-embryo can still develop into a normal colt, calf or lamb.

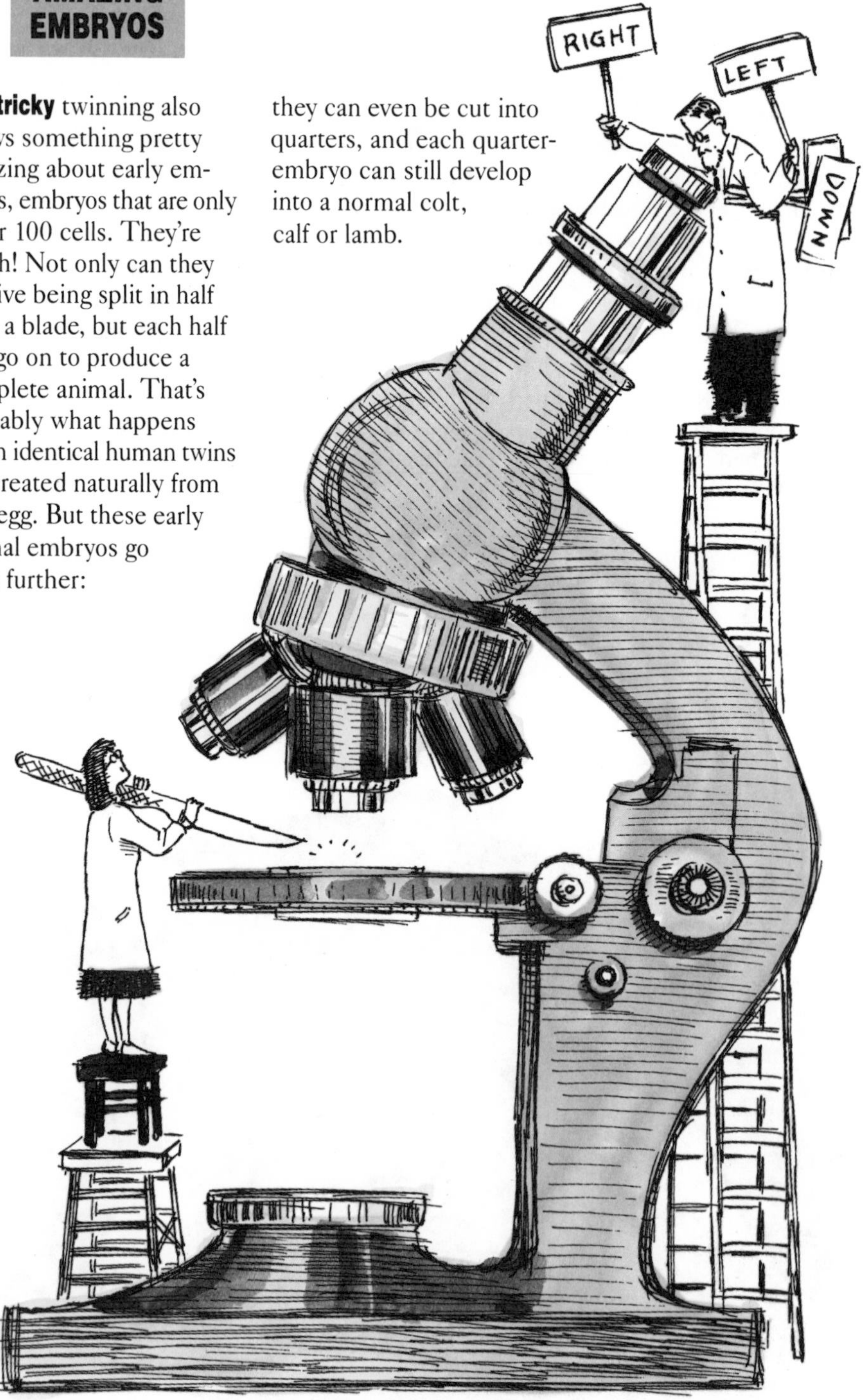

In Aldous Huxley's scary science-fiction book about the future, *Brave New World*, the science of reproduction was taken much further. Human eggs were "boka-novskified" – radiated, chilled and flooded with alcohol – to make twins of twins of twins. Sometimes 96 babies were made from a single egg. Scientists today wouldn't even think of doing what Huxley imagined in his novel more than 50 years ago. But they are helping parents to have babies in brand-new ways – and some of these babies are twins.

And in the future? Nobody's planning to "bokanovskify" human eggs, but babies may be made in ways we haven't even dreamed of yet.

CHAPTER FOUR

TWINS PLUS

We don't really need science to help us make multiple babies – we've been doing it ourselves for thousands of years. Triplets, quadruplets and quintuplets are three, four or five babies all living in the womb together and born within a few minutes of each other. If you think being a twin and having a living, breathing copy of yourself is interesting, imagine having two, three or even four copies! That could happen with triplets, quadruplets and quintuplets.

They aren't necessarily identical, though. For instance, triplets can be two identical twins and one fraternal twin. That means there were two fertilized eggs to start with, and one of them split once to produce three babies altogether. Quadruplets and quintuplets can be all kinds of combinations, from all identical to all fraternal, and almost everything in between. Apparently the only unheard-of combination is quadruplets that are two pairs of identical twins: probably the odds of having two eggs split at the same time are just too great. These groups of twins-plus are sometimes called "supertwins."

THE FAMOUS CANADIAN SUPERTWINS

The Dionne quintuplets were born in a tiny Ontario town on May 28, 1934. Quintuplets are rare enough, but the Dionnes were truly amazing, because they were identical quintuplets and they all lived. They were born on a little farm, without any of the help their mother could have had in a hospital. Even in a hospital, however, doctors in the 1930s didn't have the knowledge or the equipment that helps keep tiny babies alive today. And the Dionne quintuplets *were* tiny! The weight of all five together was just over 5 kg (11 lbs., 1½ oz.) – the size of one big baby. Their legs and

arms were finger-sized, and you could hold each one on the palm of your hand.

Even the doctor who delivered the quintuplets didn't expect them to live, but they did. The outside world found out a day later when their uncle innocently asked the editor of the nearest newspaper, "How much would it cost to insert a birth notice for five babies born at one time?" That started it, and pretty soon the Dionne quintuplets were world famous. People traveled from everywhere to the little town of Callander to see them. In fact, over the next ten years, 3 million people came.

The quints, or "quins" as they were called, were on the cover of *Modern Screen* magazine. They were called the "world's greatest news-picture story" by *Time* magazine. They posed for advertisements with slogans such as "The Dionne Quins use only Colgate Dental Cream" (those were the days before it was called toothpaste) and "How Lysol protected the Dionne Quintuplets from Infection."

There have been other sets of quintuplets born since, but none of them, as far as we know, have been identical. So the Dionne quintuplets, even today, are a unique set of people.

Up to now, quintuplets are the biggest set of "supertwins" to survive. And no wonder – the more babies a woman is carrying, the smaller they are and the sooner they're born, so the harder it is for them to survive. They're also very rare: triplets occur in North America at the rate of one in 10,000 births, and quadruplets come once in 900,000 births. Quintuplets? One in 100,000,000!

SUPERDUPERTWINS

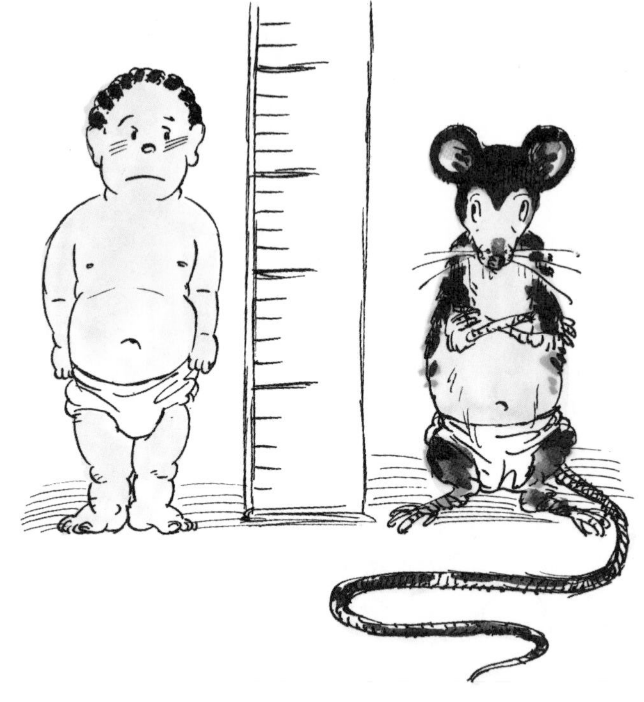

You have a better chance of winning a lottery than of having quintuplets. And as for identical quintuplets like the Dionnes – they're so rare you can't even figure out the odds. But now some of these odds might be changing.

Today doctors may give a woman fertility drugs if she wants to have a baby but hasn't been able to get pregnant. The drugs can help because they cause several eggs to be released at once from the woman's ovaries. That makes it more likely that at least one egg will be fertilized and start to develop into an embryo.

Women taking these drugs aren't *trying* to have triplets or quadruplets. It's hard enough taking care of one new baby, let alone three or four! But the catch is that sometimes more than one of the eggs is fertilized. The surprised mother finds out that not only is she going to have that long-awaited baby, but she's going to have a bunch! It doesn't happen all the time, but many of the triplets and quadruplets of recent years were born after their mothers took fertility drugs.

If you really want to stretch your imagination, try this tale of supertwins from the distant past. The story goes that in the year 1276 a Dutch countess, Margaret of Henneberg, was punished for mocking a poor mother. The punishment? She gave birth to "365 children, in bigness all like newborn mice." There were supposed to have been 182 sons, 182 daughters, and one who was in between.

Of course no one today believes this story, but it's curious that the storyteller is pretty accurate about the size of the 365 children. If they totaled about 5 kg (the total size of the Dionne quintuplets), then each child would weigh about 14 g (½ oz.), not far from the size of a newborn mouse!

Today doctors can help produce a different kind of supertwins, babies that have given a whole new meaning to the word "twins." Usually twins are born at the same time. Not exactly the same time, of course: one is a few minutes, or even a couple of hours, older than the other. But *18 months* older?

In 1987 a British doctor, Patrick Steptoe, announced the birth of one of the most unusual pairs of twins ever. The first member of the pair, Amy Wright, was born in October 1985; the second, Elizabeth Mary

Wright, arrived in April 1987. Sounds unbelievable, doesn't it? The answer to this puzzle is that the two twins were not in their mother's womb at the same time.

They were both "test-tube babies." Sperm and eggs were mixed in a laboratory dish; then one fertilized egg was put back into the mother, where it developed like a normal baby. The other tiny embryo was carefully frozen, then carefully thawed out when the mother felt she was ready for a second baby. Are Amy and Elizabeth actually twins? In one way they're not, because they weren't in the womb together. But they *did* come from eggs that were fertilized at the same time, like all fraternal twins.

The 96 science-fiction twins of Aldous Huxley's *Brave New World* were born at industrial "incubation" centers. And while these imaginary babies would have begun their lives just like today's test-tube babies, in *Brave New World* the multiple twins were never put into a woman's womb. They spent the entire nine months of pregnancy in special laboratory vats. When they were "born," they were made to measure for whatever the government wanted them to do. Even though Huxley wrote *Brave New World* in 1932, it's still a scary book today, and it shows what evil people could do if they were free to use science and medicine any way they liked.

TWINS OF THE DISTANT FUTURE

In the 1970s scientists were shocked when a book called *In His Image: The Cloning of a Man* appeared. It was supposed to be the true story of the first cloning of a human. If it was true, the cloning would have been a spectacular scientific first: a technique that would have made it possible for anyone to create his or her own twin.

If you wanted to make a clone of yourself, here's how it might be done. First, doctors would have to do microscopic surgery on a single human egg cell, removing all the genes. Then they would take some of your own cells, by simply scraping the inside of your cheek. They'd put the full set of genes from one of your cells into the vacant egg cell. It would be very, very tricky. But if that egg cell with your genes in it were put into a woman's womb, the baby that would be born would be your identical twin, only many years younger.

Just think of it: it would be one of the strangest experiences you could imagine. As you watched that baby grow up, it would be like watching yourself grow up again. Or would it? That baby would not have the same experiences you did, or the same friends,

and probably wouldn't even live in the same house with the same parents. Worst of all, you probably wouldn't be able to resist butting in and telling your clone what to do and what not to do. ("I remember when I grew up, I always did my homework on Friday nights . . .") Your clone could never end up being exactly the same as you.

Today, most experts think that the book *In His Image* was fiction, not fact – but some of those people weren't so sure at first.

After all, cloning is possible; it has been done with frogs and mice. But so far, there's no evidence from any lab in the world that a human clone has been created. No evidence other than the book, and the author is not talking.

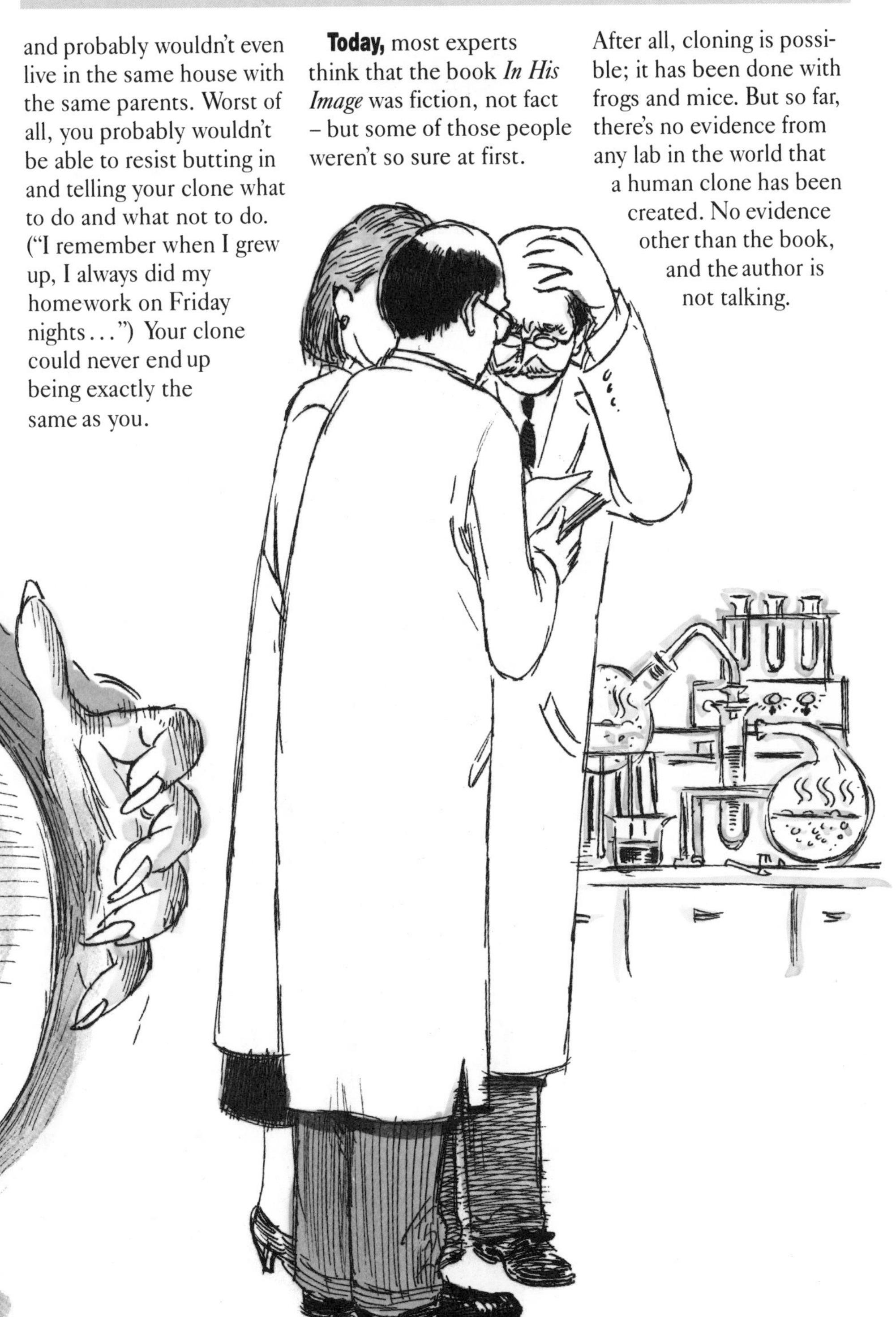

THE STRANGEST TWIN OF ALL

The strangest twin of all is a woman in Vienna who is a combination of two twins! She was discovered by accident when doctors found that her children had blood types they couldn't have inherited from her. Your blood type is determined by your parents' genes, so this woman and her children were a real puzzle. It was as if the children had somehow inherited their blood type from their mother's sister. But she didn't have any sisters.

The explanation is that the woman must have been a twin when she was an embryo in her mother's womb. But her fraternal twin embryo didn't develop into a separate baby. Instead, the two embryos merged into one, an embryo that became a kind of patchwork quilt of the two, including some of the tissues of one and some of the other. That's why the children had blood types so different from their mother's: they inherited their blood cells from the "other" twin.

CHAPTER FOUR

Amazing Coincidences

Our close resemblance turned the tide
Of my domestic life
For somehow, my intended bride
Became my brother's wife.

In fact, year after year the same
Absurd mistakes went on,
And when I died, the neighbors came
And buried brother John.

enry Sambrooke Leigh wrote that poem more than 100 years ago. Obviously telling identical twins apart has been giving people trouble for a long time!

CHAPTER FIVE

It's not just that identical twins look the same. If you don't know them really well, sometimes it's even harder to tell them apart because they often act the same way, right down to the little details of how they shrug their shoulders or wave their hands. If you know twins, you've probably seen that they're similar in more than just their looks. But that shouldn't be surprising: after all, twins know each other very well. They've grown up together in the same house with the same parents, they usually go to the same schools and they probably have the same friends. It's not just that they started out together in the womb; they've lived similar lives since then too.

But there are some identical twins who have grown up totally apart from each other. For instance, each infant may have been adopted by a different family. Sometimes separated twins end up in different cities or even in different countries. What happens if they grow up apart, not even realizing that they have twin brothers or sisters? Do twins with completely different homes, different parents and friends, even different jobs still act the same, like the same things and talk the same way? Or do different surroundings make "identical" twins different?

There are now some answers for these questions. Several sets of identical twins separated at birth have been found, and they've volunteered to take part in studies to see just how similar they are.

CHAPTER FIVE

THE TWO JIMS

Jim Lewis and Jim Springer are probably the most famous of the twins that were separated most of their lives. Jim and Jim were adopted when they were just four weeks old (and by chance they were given the same first name by their two sets of parents). They were apart for the next 39 years. But even though each grew up never knowing about the other, they turned out to have some unbelievable similarities.

Both Jims enjoy carpentry. They cross their legs the same way. Each built a little white bench around the one tree in his front yard. Both have vacationed on the same three-block-long stretch of beach in Florida. Both drive Chevrolets and like doing household chores. Both have had dogs named Toy. Both have been divorced; both their first wives were named Linda, and both their second wives were named Betty. Both Jims chew their fingernails. Both suddenly put on the same amount of weight at the same age, for no apparent reason. They drink the same brand of beer.

They have the same pulse rate, the same blood pressure and the same kind of headaches. In fact, they even describe their headaches the same way. Springer says, "It feels like somebody's hitting you in the back of the neck with a two-by-four." Lewis's version: "It's centered in the back of my neck and it nearly knocks me out sometimes."

The Jims aren't the only twins with a remarkable history. Daphne and Barbara, separated for 41 years, are British twins with the same kind of story. They both love blue. Both fear heights, and they hold onto the banister when they're walking down stairs because they're afraid of falling. Both have a habit of pushing up their noses, which they both call "squidging," and they go on fad diets all the time. And perhaps most amazing of all, in the year 1960 only, both Daphne and Barbara kept diaries. The two diaries were even exactly the same make and color.

COFFEE AND SNAKES

There are many other pairs of identical twins that have lived apart, like the Jim twins and Barbara and Daphne, and most of these twins have their own stories to tell. Some of the habits they share can be as strange as liking to sneeze loudly in crowds as a joke. (The twins who share that habit also flush the toilet before they use it, keep rubber bands on their wrists and dip buttered toast in their coffee.)

How can these amazing coincidences be explained? You might not be surprised if twins who had lived together were this similar. It's easy to pick up the same habits and the same likes and dislikes if you're living in the same house. But why are these twins

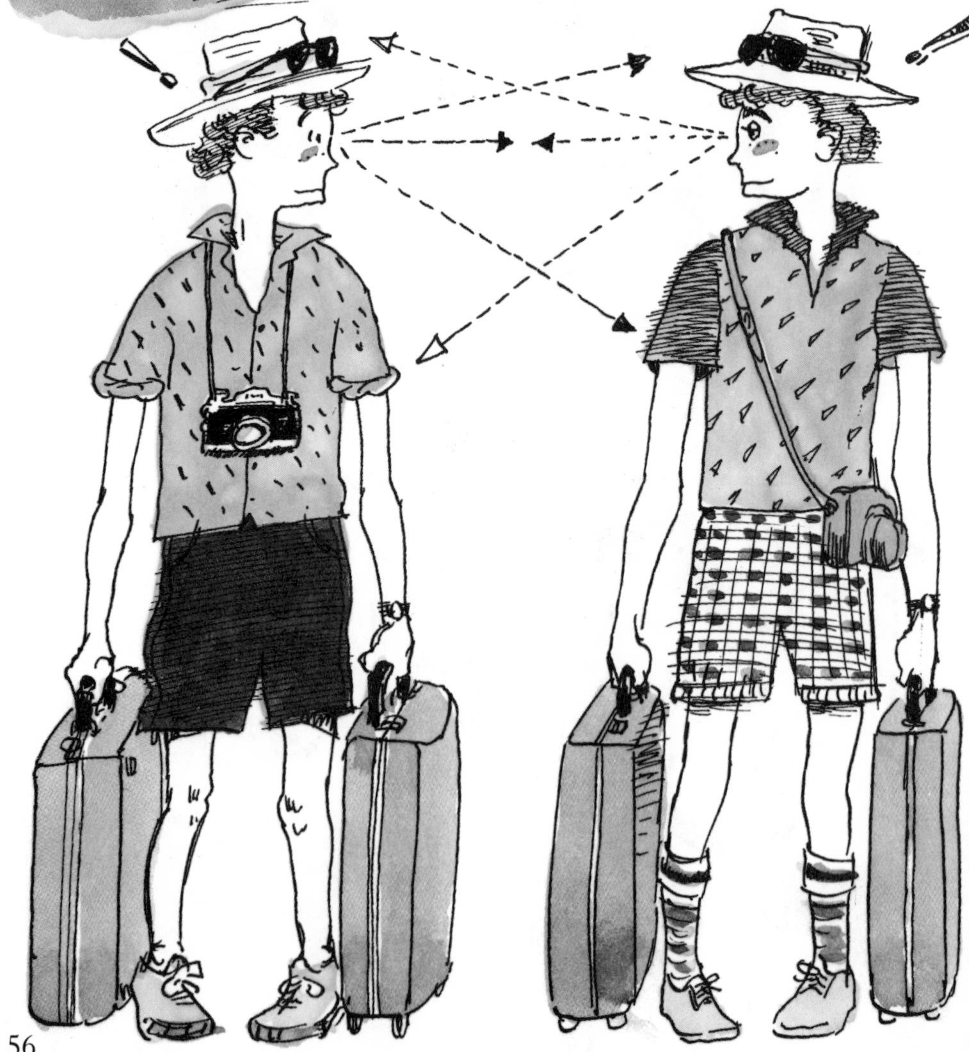

who've lived apart so similar, and in such special ways?

It is possible that some of it is just plain coincidence. The two Jims drive Chevrolets – but so do lots of other people, so that doesn't really count. Maybe vacationing in Florida is the natural thing for both Jims to do with the time and money they have. In fact, a study at a Virginia university showed that sometimes the same kinds of coincidences show up in the lives of people who aren't related at all.

Two girls in this study were both Baptists. They listed volleyball and tennis as their favorite sports and English and math as their favorite subjects. Both preferred vacationing at historic places. They were both studying nursing too, but they weren't even distantly related. You probably have friends who are a lot like you too: they might prefer the same sports, like the same TV shows and read the same magazines as you. But it doesn't mean there is a strange twin bond between you.

People don't even have to know each other to appear to share a common bond. Here's an example: about 45 percent of all people fear snakes, and 55 percent drink coffee. If somebody said to you, "Look at these amazing twins – both of them drink coffee and are afraid of snakes," you might be impressed. But you shouldn't be: about 25 percent of all people have both those traits anyway.

CHAPTER FIVE

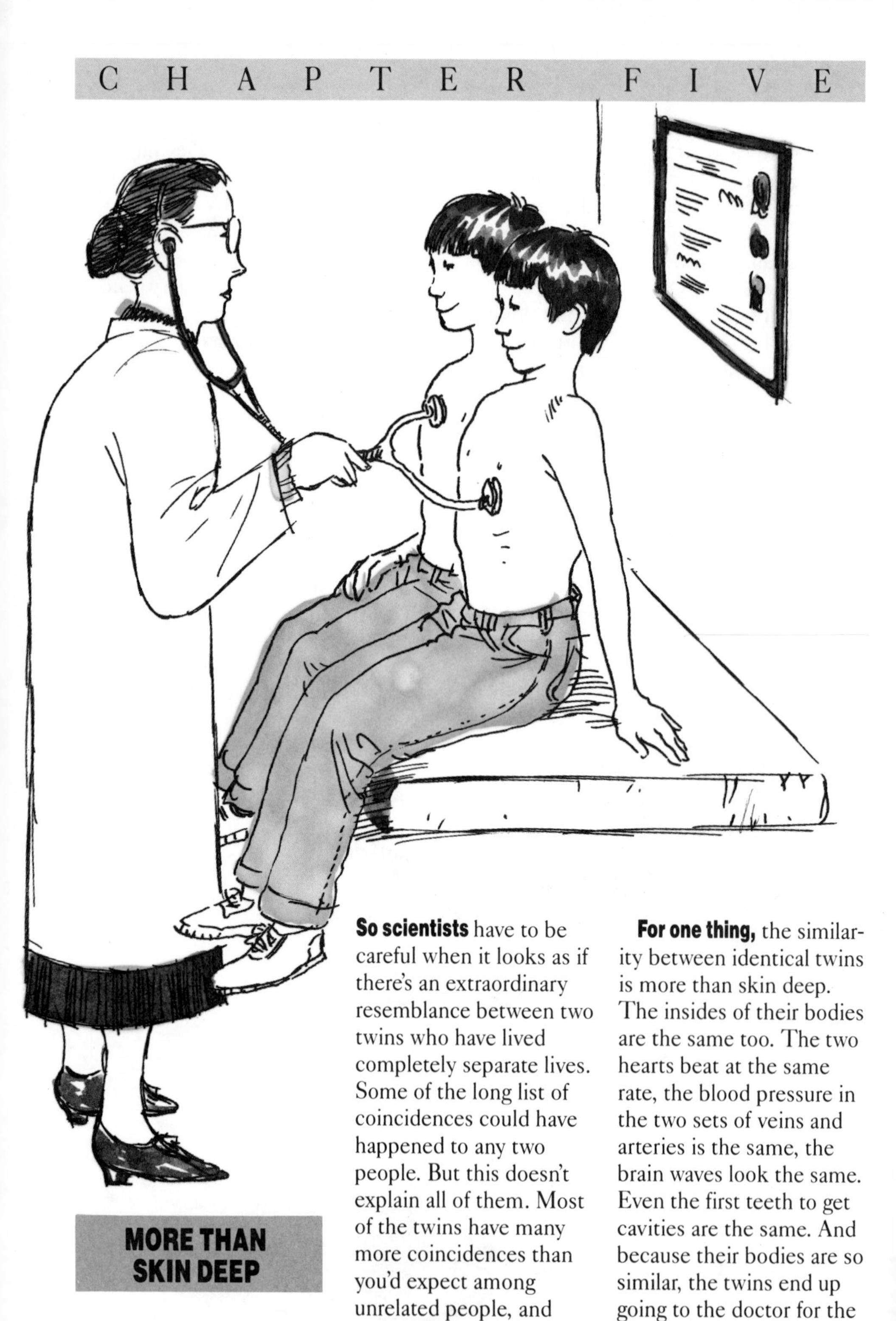

MORE THAN SKIN DEEP

So scientists have to be careful when it looks as if there's an extraordinary resemblance between two twins who have lived completely separate lives. Some of the long list of coincidences could have happened to any two people. But this doesn't explain all of them. Most of the twins have many more coincidences than you'd expect among unrelated people, and some of them are very special coincidences.

For one thing, the similarity between identical twins is more than skin deep. The insides of their bodies are the same too. The two hearts beat at the same rate, the blood pressure in the two sets of veins and arteries is the same, the brain waves look the same. Even the first teeth to get cavities are the same. And because their bodies are so similar, the twins end up going to the doctor for the same reasons, at the same time.

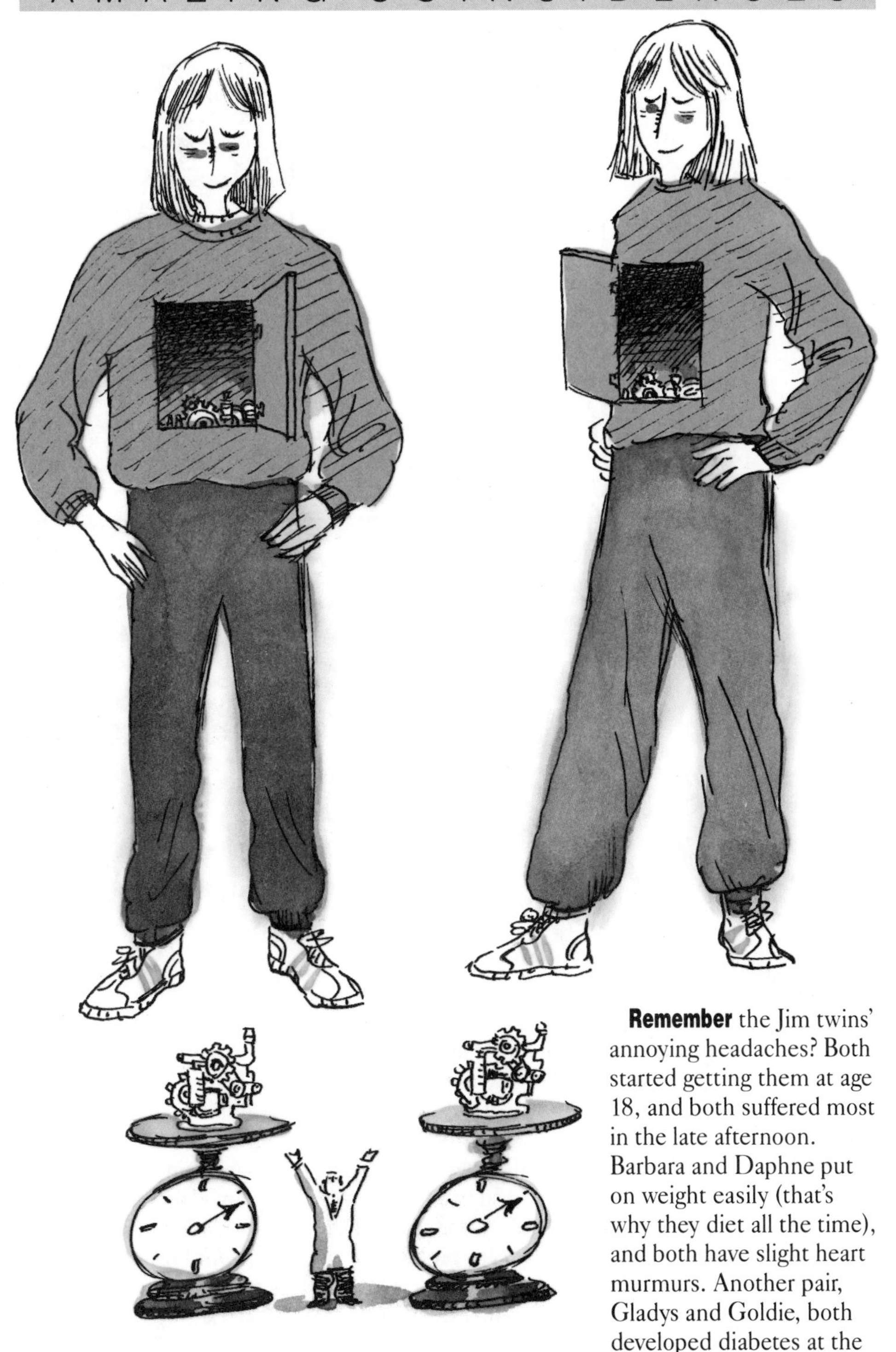

Remember the Jim twins' annoying headaches? Both started getting them at age 18, and both suffered most in the late afternoon. Barbara and Daphne put on weight easily (that's why they diet all the time), and both have slight heart murmurs. Another pair, Gladys and Goldie, both developed diabetes at the same time.

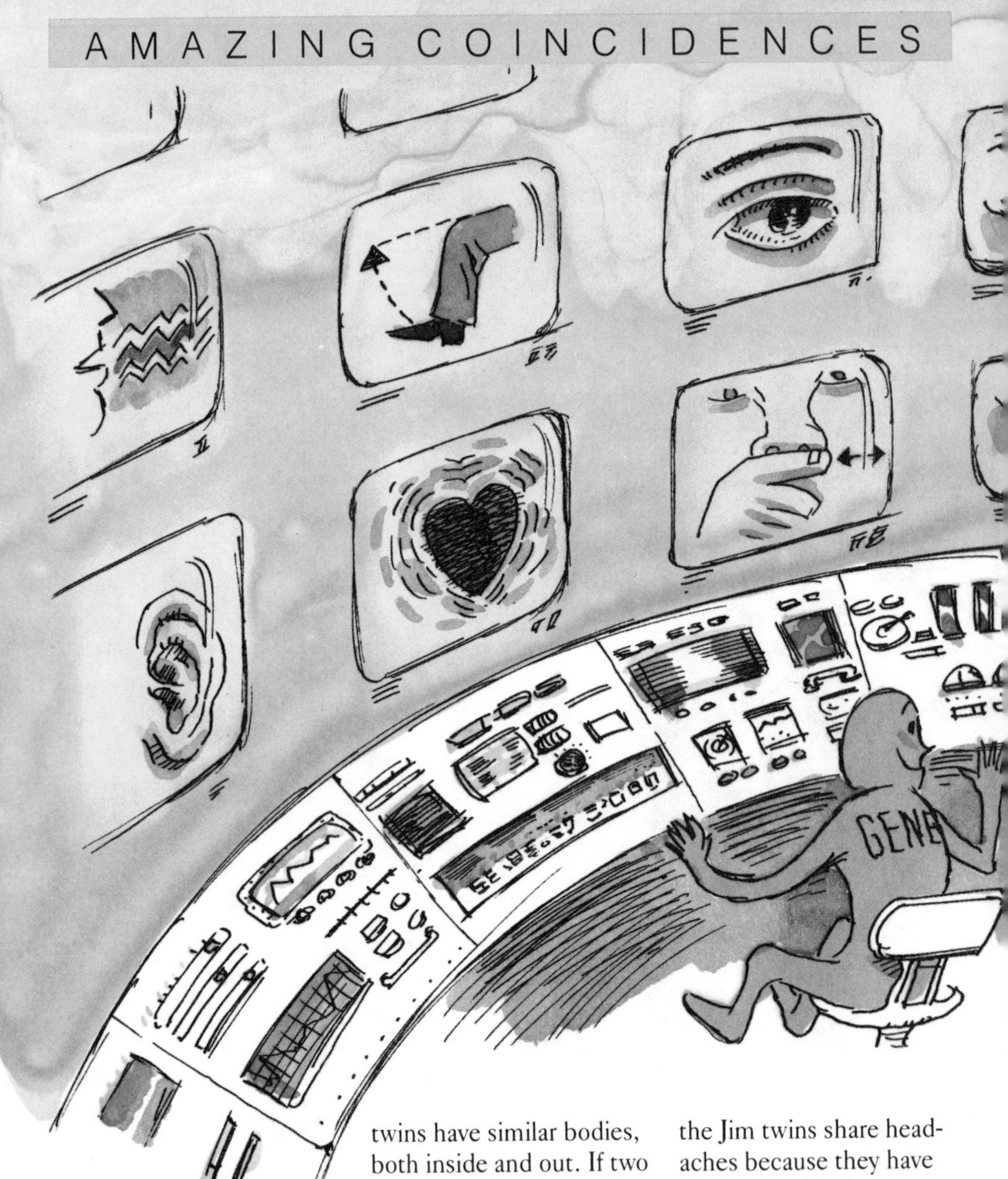

Scientists aren't really surprised by these medical coincidences, and they don't see anything uncanny about them. They're used to the idea that identical twins have similar bodies, both inside and out. If two bodies are the same, from the size of the bones to the amounts of different kinds of body chemicals, then those two bodies will probably share some of the same health problems. For instance, if twins can't make insulin properly, they'll both get diabetes, like Gladys and Goldie. Maybe the Jim twins share headaches because they have problems with the way their blood circulates. Even the way Barbara and Daphne gain weight could be blamed on their identical sets of genes – somehow they don't burn the calories off fast enough.

But it is surprising that twins are so similar in the way they think and act.

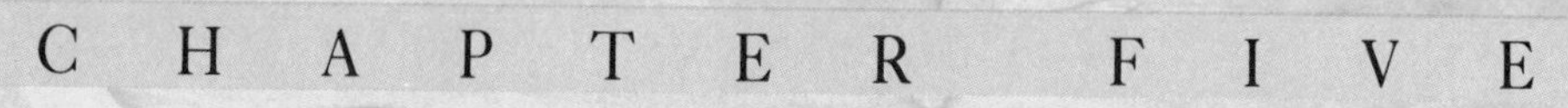

CHAPTER FIVE

Dorothy and Bridget, from England, both wave as they speak, sometimes covering their mouths as they do. They also push back the cuticles of their fingernails while they're talking. When they met for the first time, each was wearing seven rings.

James and Robert both tap the table with a finger when they are talking, and both flick their fingers when they can't think of an answer right away. Alfred and Harry both nod the same way when they speak, and each closes his eyes as he turns his head. Another pair of twins were both great story-tellers, even though one was well educated and the other hardly educated at all.

An odd habit like flicking your fingers seems to be something you just pick up when you're young, maybe from your parents or your friends in school. But then why would two people who have lived their whole lives apart both do it?

When twins have special little habits that are exactly the same, scientists now think it's likely that their identical genes are responsible. So not only do twins' genes make them look the same, in some ways they make them act the same too. And even think the same!

WHERE DID YOU GET THAT TEMPER?

At the University of Minnesota, psychologists are studying identical twins who grew up apart. They've already found some fascinating things. For instance, identical twins often score closer to each other on intelligence tests than *you* would if *you* wrote the same test twice in a row. On these tests the twins score as if they were practically sharing the same brain.

The twins might help answer a tough question: what's more important in forming your personality, the genes you inherit from your parents or the experiences you have? If the quick-tempered movie star has a son with the same temper, was the son born with it or did he learn it? Let's say you're able to stay

very calm in emergencies, when everyone else is getting panicky. Your mother is the same way. Did you inherit your mother's calm, or did you learn it by watching her?

The identical twins raised apart have exactly the same genes but completely different experiences. So if both twins have a bad temper, it's possible that they inherited the genes that make a bad temper more likely. But if only one of them is hot tempered, then genes probably don't control temper – it must be experiences that are responsible for making one twin easygoing and the other cranky. By studying the twins, psychologists hope to learn which personality traits in everybody are controlled mostly by our genes, and which depend more on the experiences we've all had.

The Minnesota tests haven't been completed yet, but so far they show what most people expected: nothing in the twins' personalities is formed completely by genes *or* completely by experience. Both have a role, but it seems that inheritance is more important in your personality than many scientists used to believe.

Do you like being the center of attention? Do you obey rules and always do what your parents and your teachers tell you? Do you worry a lot and get upset easily? Believe it or not, all of these personality traits may owe more to your genes than to your upbringing. You could have inherited the tendency to be like that. So if you fit any of those descriptions, you have your parents' genes to thank for a good part of it. Even something so personal as having a vivid imagination may have more to do with genes than with what you've learned in school.

What does this all mean? If you're born with a tendency to worry, are you going to worry the rest of your life? Will you always want to be the focus of attention if that's written in your genes? Not necessarily. Your genes are really just a rough sketch of what you might turn out to be. It's up to you to fill in the details of the picture yourself.

CHAPTER FIVE

CHAPTER FIVE

The twins in these studies have helped us all by volunteering to take part in scientists' research. But think of how eerie it must have been for them to suddenly meet replicas of themselves! Stop right now and imagine that you have a twin somewhere, a twin that has the same hobbies as you do, likes the same clothes and music and even talks the same way. How do you think you'd get along with your newfound twin?

The happy part of this story is that most of these twins, when they finally meet, get along pretty well.

They don't all keep seeing their twins regularly, but for some it's changed their lives, because they now have another "self" to share their lives with.

The identical twins raised by separate families have amazed everyone who's talked to them or seen them. They're alike in so many ways that they're even more "identical" than twins who live together. That may seem really strange, because you'd expect twins raised together, with the same experiences, to be more alike themselves. But they're not.

It may be that identical twins raised together try to be a little different from each other. They avoid competing. So if one twin is good right away at running, the other twin will turn to something else rather than be second best. If one twin always wants to run the show, the other twin will give in. If one twin gets her ears pierced, the other won't. Often their parents may encourage them to be different from each other. But identical twins who aren't raised together are free to be themselves, and so they actually turn out to be more alike.

Twins Around the World

In Alexandre Dumas's novel The Man in the Iron Mask, *the identical twin brother of King Louis XIV of France is doomed to spend his life in a dungeon. Why? When the twins were born, their father feared there would be conflict over which of the two should be king, so he hid one away. One boy became Louis XIV, the Sun King. His twin brother's face was covered with an iron mask so that even his jailers wouldn't know the king had a twin.*

C H A P T E R S I X

The Man in the Iron Mask is fiction, but the problem of deciding which twin in a royal family becomes king or queen can be tricky. In countries where there are still kings and queens, a court official is usually present when the queen gives birth so that he can record which twin was born first. In some countries in the past, the solution was much more brutal: one of the twins would be killed, so there would be no question of who would eventually take the throne.

CHAPTER SIX

Today in most countries in the world the birth of twins is an exciting event. The mother and father worry about having to buy two sets of clothes, changing two sets of diapers, and doing twice as much work, but most of the time they have twice as much fun too.

TWINS AROUND THE WORLD

But the birth of twins wasn't always so simple. We know now that twins are the result of an egg splitting in half, or of two different eggs developing at the same time. But before people knew this, they had to decide for themselves why twins were born, and what the arrival of two children at the same time meant. Anywhere you look in the world over the centuries, there have been stories, myths and traditions about twins. Some peoples welcomed twins and loved them; some feared twins and even killed them.

Many Indian tribes in North America had gods who were twins. Some thought that twins controlled the weather. The Tsimshian Indians on the west coast of Canada called the wind "the breath of twins." The Mojave Indians thought that twins came from the sky, using thunder and lightning to come down to earth. If lightning struck near the house of a pregnant woman, the Mojave thought twins were likely to be the result. The Akwaala tribe of southern California felt that having twins was a rare privilege. They believed that the spirits of twins lived in the mountains and that some of these spirits occasionally reached the world by being born to a human mother.

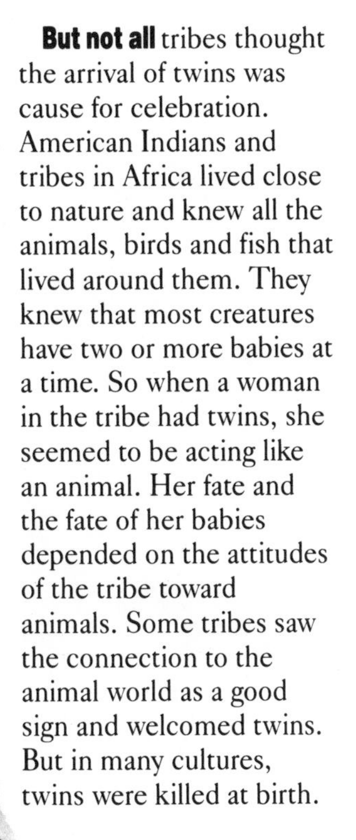

But not all tribes thought the arrival of twins was cause for celebration. American Indians and tribes in Africa lived close to nature and knew all the animals, birds and fish that lived around them. They knew that most creatures have two or more babies at a time. So when a woman in the tribe had twins, she seemed to be acting like an animal. Her fate and the fate of her babies depended on the attitudes of the tribe toward animals. Some tribes saw the connection to the animal world as a good sign and welcomed twins. But in many cultures, twins were killed at birth.

The Kwakiutl Indians live on the west coast of Canada. They're one of the Indian tribes who carve totem poles. The birth of twins was a big event in the Kwakiutl tradition because all twins were thought to have supernatural powers. And twins of the same sex were believed to be salmon that had taken the form of children. Birth marks on the children were assumed to be scars left by harpoons that had hit them when they were salmon. It was considered foolish and dangerous to take twins too close to the water, for fear that they would be changed back into salmon!

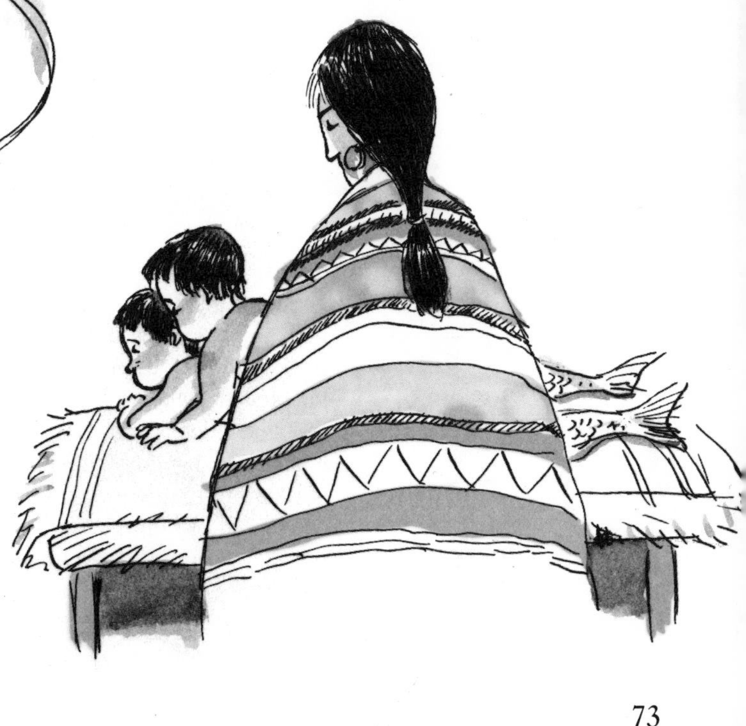

CHAPTER SIX

It's hard if you're not a Kwakiutl to realize just how important the salmon were in the traditional tribal myths. Salmon were thought to live in houses, just as humans do, in cities at the bottom of the ocean. And when the salmon swam upstream to lay their eggs and die, the Kwakiutl believed that their souls were released to return to the sea.

The Kwakiutl thought that salmon possessed great magical and spiritual powers. It's no wonder that twins, who were salmon in the form of children, have always been very important to the Kwakiutl. Just as the salmon turn red as they swim upstream and die, Kwakiutl twins were painted red, and they wore rings of red cedar bark and white feathers in their hair.

Kwakiutl twins were also thought to have supernatural powers, especially in relation to the weather. If the elders wanted better weather, the twins were dressed up and taken outside. If the Kwakiutl wanted rain – perhaps because the rivers were too low to allow the salmon to run upstream – the twins' bodies were painted black and red and their hair was oiled before they were taken outside. Twins could cause fogs to disappear and wind to begin just by a wave of the hand. Because they were really salmon, they could even invite their fellow fish to swim upstream, where the Kwakiutl fishermen could catch them.

Other tribes in the interior of British Columbia, including the Thompson Indians, believed that twins had a magical connection to grizzly bears. The Thompsons called twins "grizzly bear children" and thought that they were under special grizzly protection. The twins' father would even sing the song of the grizzly when the twins were bathing! The grizzly connection might have come from the fact that grizzly bears usually give birth to twins themselves. Whatever the reason, it would be hard to find a more impressive protector for twins than the grizzly bear. It's sad to realize that today, as many of the twin traditions have died out, these twins' great "protector," the grizzly, has almost died out too. Grizzlies just can't live near civilization.

The British Columbia Indians thought the spirit world was as real as the world they saw around them, and that animals were just as important as humans. To them, twins were important connections to those other animals, so they were treated with love and respect.

On the other hand, until this century, twins in Japan were treated with anything but love and respect. The Japanese used to think the

birth of twins was a disaster. They didn't come right out and say it, but their distaste for twins probably came from the feeling that having twins was something only animals should do. Unlike the North American Indians, the Japanese didn't like the association with animals.

In the 1700s and 1800s, a twin birth was kept completely quiet. Anyone who happened to be present when twins were born in the house of someone important, like a feudal lord, had to swear never to tell anyone. The penalty for breaking that oath was death!

CHAPTER SIX

Usually if male twins were born to a lord, one of the lord's courtiers would adopt one twin to raise as his own. But that twin would also take with him some badge or token of who he really was, so that if his twin brother died, he could replace him as the rightful heir to his father's title.

Deciding which male twin to give away and which one to keep created some problems. You might think it would make sense for the lord to keep the first-born, but what if he was weaker and not as healthy? In that case the lord would probably want the second child

to be his heir. But the lords and their courtiers were much too polite to crowd around the cradle saying, "This one's heavier!" "But no, look here, this one's got better color!" They had to have some honorable reason for choosing the healthier-looking twin.

A doctor named Kakuryo Katakura, writing 200 years ago, had it all figured out. He said it was obvious that one of the twins was the host in the womb, and the other was the guest. Guests are treated very well in Japan, so the bigger, healthier twin was obviously the guest. Katakura didn't actually say whether the guest or the host was kept as the child of the lord, but you can bet it was the guest.

So, strange as it seems, on the east side of the Pacific Ocean, in British Columbia, the birth of twins brought rejoicing. Across the ocean, it brought nothing but worry and unhappiness. But to find the most elaborate and interesting beliefs and rituals about twins, we have to go to Africa.

Eighteen million Nigerians belong to a tribe called the Yoruba. Today they live everywhere from tiny villages to big modern cities. Of all the people in the world, the Yoruba have the most interesting traditions about twins. They are, after all, the people who until recently were having twins at the incredible rate of one pair for every 22 births. (See page 23.) When you have that many twins, they're bound to become an important part of your life.

The legends say that centuries ago the Yoruba used to kill twins when they were born, or they would banish the mother and her children, partly because they thought having two children was animal-like. There are even stories of "twin towns," where banished mothers and their children were free to live. Sometimes mothers could return, even occasionally with one twin, but usually the twins and their mother were banished forever.

Happily, this brutal treatment has changed dramatically into a kind of fascination with twins. The Yoruba have traditional names for twins: the first-born is called Taiwo ("the one who tastes the world"), and the second Kehinde ("the one who lags behind"), whether they're boys or girls. These are traditional names – Yoruba twins today have modern names too.

Curiously, the second-born is considered to be the older, more senior twin. The Yoruba explain it by

saying that Kehinde sends Taiwo into the world first to scout it out and see what it's like before Kehinde follows.

If a Yoruba twin dies, the mother goes to a sculptor and has a little doll made that represents her dead child. This little wooden doll is decorated with bracelets around the arms or ankles. The bereaved mother keeps the doll with her and treats it as if it is her dead child. She dresses it, brushes food against its lips, even dances with it.

The Yoruba tradition says that twins share a soul. If one twin dies, it might cause the other twin to die also, to bring the two half-souls together again. So the mother cares for the dead twin to prevent the death of her living twin..

The Yoruba are convinced that twins exist as spirits. Some twin spirits have not yet been born, some are currently living as human twins, and others have returned from human life to the spirit world. They are powerful spirits too: not only can they lure a living twin back to the spirit world, but they can also prevent the mother from having any more children if she doesn't take care of the doll.

You may think that these beliefs have nothing to do with what people think about twins where you live. But think about the endless stories of links between twins' minds – how twins can read each other's thoughts, for instance. Is that so different from believing that twins share a soul?

Twin Telepathy?

he brothers were scarcely conscious of it themselves, but telepathy was a common occurrence in their lives, and when one returned home the other was always aware of it while his brother was still several streets away."

Thornton Wilder, who wrote those words in his novel *The Bridge of San Luis Rey*, knew what twins could do – he was a twin himself. In his story each twin is eerily aware of what the other is thinking. This sense – called telepathy – is the quality of twins that is the most fascinating, the hardest to believe, and the one that drives scientists absolutely nuts.

CHAPTER SEVEN

CHAPTER SEVEN

There are hundreds of reports of twins reading each other's minds, but unfortunately twins don't seem to do it when scientists are there, recording what goes on. On the other hand, so many twins have reported that one can sense what the other is doing that it's hard to ignore them. Here's one account, first told by Charles Crail in his book *My Twin Joe*.

TWIN TELEPATHY?

A teacher suspected that Charles and his twin brother Joe were cheating on exams, because they always wrote the same answers, right or wrong, even when they were sitting on opposite sides of the room. So the teacher decided to put Joe in the principal's office for the next exam. On exam day, Charles sat in the class-room with the exam in front of him, but he didn't start when everyone else did. "I'm not ready," he said, and continued to wait.

Then the principal came in and asked for an exam paper to give to Joe. He'd been busy with something else. Joe was still waiting for his exam paper in the principal's office. You guessed it: as soon as Joe got his exam, both twins started writing. Their exam papers turned out to be exactly the same: the same right answers and the same mis-takes. It was as if they were sharing the same brain.

That story is one of those that can't be proven to be true. But there are others like it. In the French army during World War I there were twin generals, Félix and Théodore Brett. They were so similar in their thinking when they were military students that the head of the French War College ordered an inquiry, because their exam papers were so much alike. The twins were cleared of cheating. Sounds a lot like Charles and Joe, doesn't it? Again, the problem with proving the story is that we don't know just how much alike those exam papers were.

Fifteen-year-old Brian Blackett was walking by himself near London, England, on Thursday, October 13, 1960. He suddenly became scared. At that very moment, on the other side of the city,

CHAPTER SEVEN

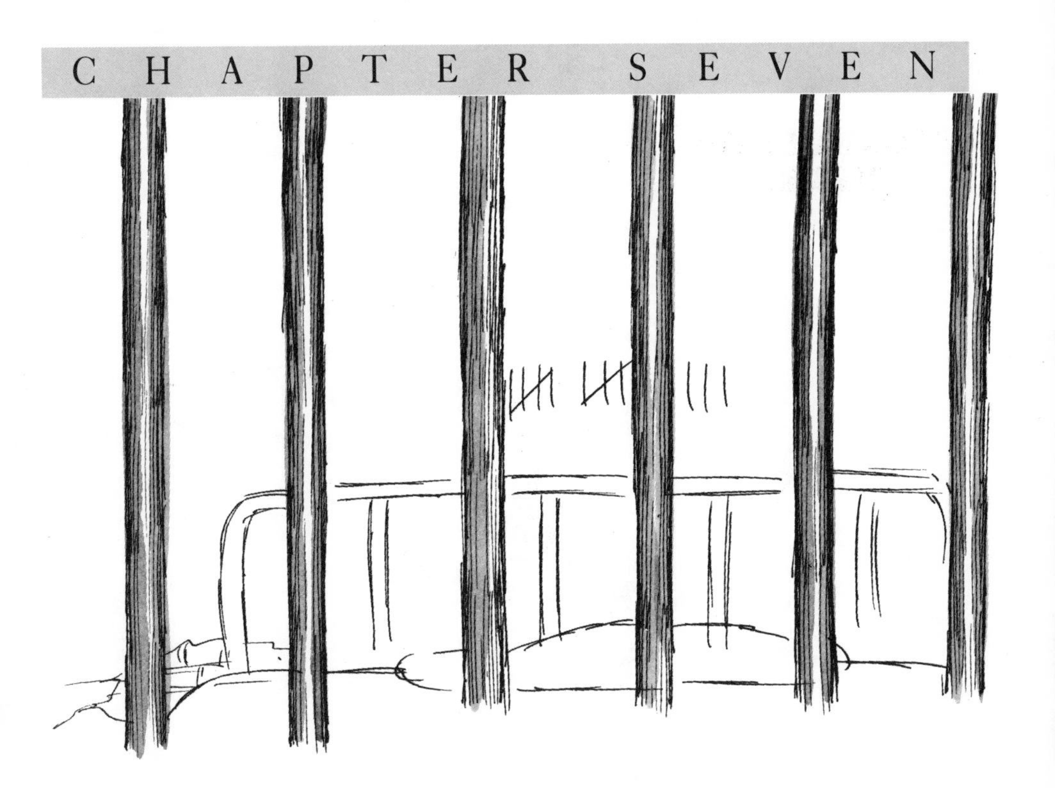

his twin brother Lennie was being sentenced to prison for breaking into a house. Brian had had no idea that Lennie was being sentenced that day.

Then there was Barbara Morgan, who got labor pains when her twin Gillian was having a baby. Kenneth Main felt sharp pains in his chest at 12:15 P.M., November 13, 1958, the exact time when his brother Keith was having a heart operation.

BRAIN WAVES AND DREAMS

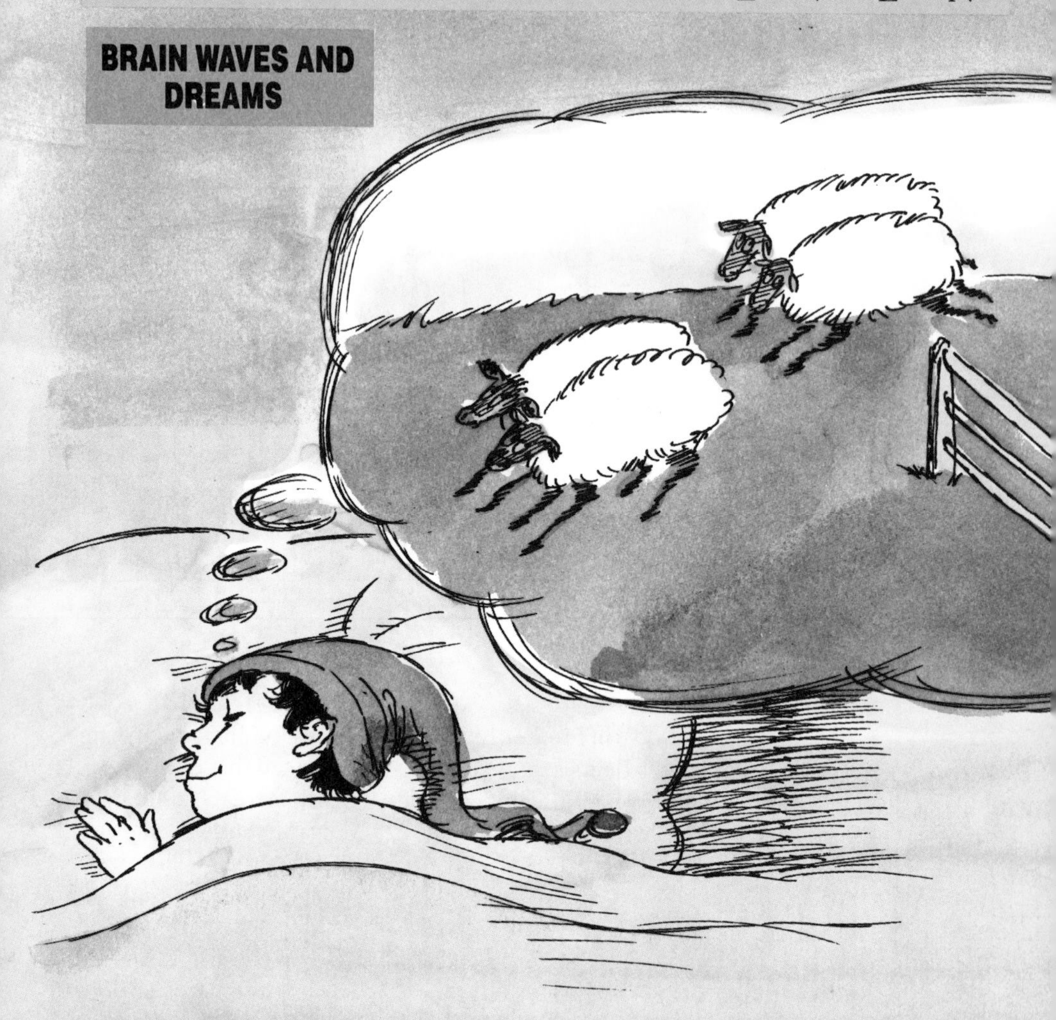

There are many more stories like this, but they all share the same weakness – it's hard to know, years later, just how accurate they are. But if even some of them are true, it means some twins can actually communicate with each other – mind to mind – without talking, and sometimes over great distances. Can twins read each other's minds? If anyone could prove they can, it would be a sensational discovery.

Maybe part of the answer is that twins' brains can be very much alike. There are some startling bits of evidence that twins' brains are so similar that they think almost identically. Their results on IQ tests can be almost identical, and their brain-wave patterns are just about the same.

Brain waves are pulses or bursts of electricity that go through your brain when you're thinking. Measuring them can't tell you what thoughts someone is having, but they do give you an idea of how the brain is processing those thoughts.

Reading brain-wave patterns is a little like

looking at city lights from an airplane. It would be pretty hard to see the exact moment when the corner store turns its lights off. But you could see that the light patterns in the city change from time to time, and you could tell that each city's pattern is different. Twins' brain waves would look like two cities with exactly the same pattern of lights.

French researchers have now discovered that IQ tests and brain waves are only part of the story. They have found by looking at those same electrical brain-wave patterns that twins share the same dream habits. They don't necessarily dream the same dreams (although some twins say they do), but they do dream at the same times of night, for about the same length of time. If you're not a twin, you don't share your dream patterns with anybody else.

None of this scientific evidence is good enough to prove that twins can read each other's minds. But these brain-wave measurements do show that even though brains are very complicated, twins' brains are amazingly alike.

A SPECIAL BOND

There are twins who think too much like each other. Greta and Freda Chaplin are English twins who have been described as having "one mind in two bodies." They talk in unison, dress alike and sleep in the same bed. When they make breakfast, they both hold onto the handle of the frying pan at the same time. Some scientists have said that the Chaplin twins are the closest thing they've ever seen to telepathy: reading each other's minds. They do so many things together that they seem to be communicating in secret ways.

C H A P T E R   S E V E N

Many twins feel that they have a special kind of bond with each other – a relationship that other people don't have. Sometimes it makes them act as if they were one person instead of two. There's a story about little twin girls who were very upset. One was crying, one was not. When the dry-eyed twin was asked why she wasn't crying, she said, "Sister's crying, so I don't need to." But the people who know the Chaplin twins feel sorry for them, because their extreme closeness has left them almost completely alone. It keeps them from having anything like a normal life: for instance, they can't hold jobs because they refuse to be apart, even for a second.

THE CALCULATOR TWINS

One of the most fascinating pairs of twins ever studied show that every once in a while, twin brains can really work as one. Charles and George are called "the calculator twins." They are identical twins who, even though they have severe mental handicaps, have an incredible memory and talent for numbers. You wouldn't believe anyone could do the things they can do, but several researchers have seen it happen.

The twins can remember any day in their lives and tell you whether it was sunny, cloudy or rainy. Mention any date in the last 40,000 years, or even the *next* 40,000 years, and within a second or two, they'll tell you what day of the week it was, or will be. One of their aunts, who worked in a law office, used to call George to check the dates of important legal documents. You can even ask them a question like "In what months in the year 2002 will the first day fall on a Friday?" You'll get the right answer: March, February and November.

In the few seconds it takes Charles and George to answer these questions, there just isn't enough time to calculate the answer with formulas and charts. And even if there were enough time, these twins aren't good enough in math to do it. Somehow the answers just come into their heads. You could say they see it in their mind's eye. Empty a bag of coins on the table, and within seconds they can tell you how many there are. "A hundred and eleven." Again, not enough time passes for them to have counted them, and in fact, they say they don't count them. They can only add and subtract a little, and they don't understand multiplication or division.

How do they do it? These amazing twins must somehow be able to see numbers in their minds, maybe in the same way that other people see pictures. There's no way of knowing exactly what the twins see

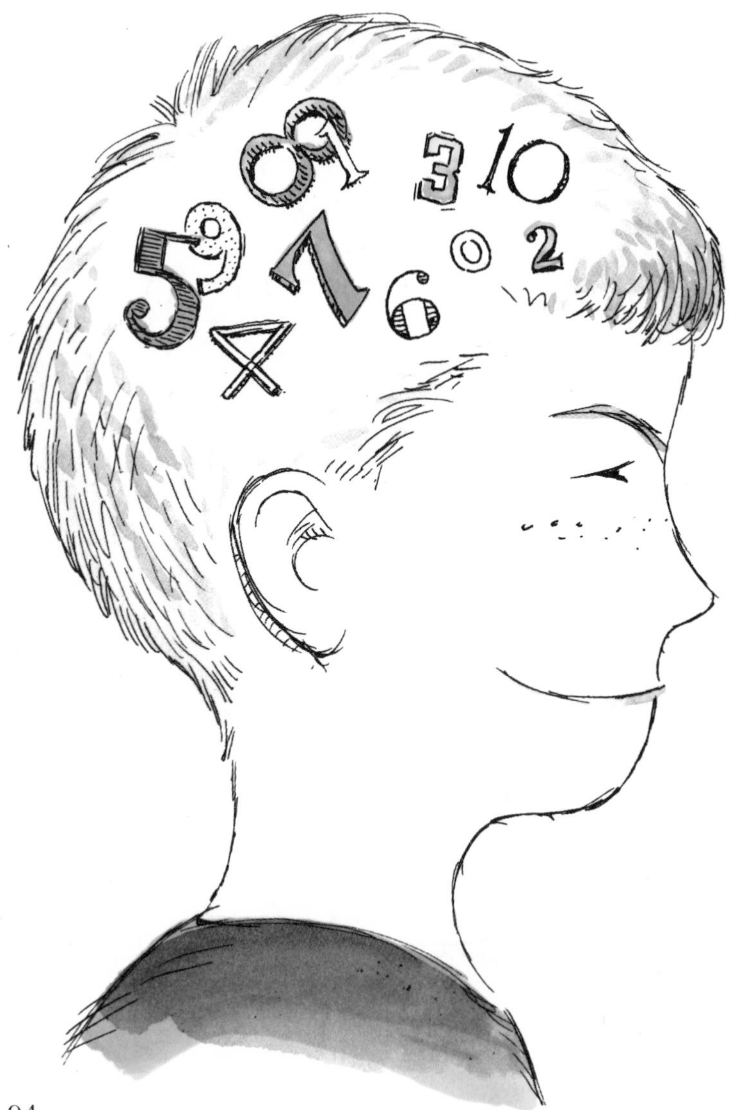

because they can't tell us. Their unusual talent does show, however, that even when the human brain is below average in some ways, it can still have some uncanny abilities that we can't even begin to explain.

What does Charles and George's story tell us about twins' brains? Every once in a while one person shows up who can perform these incredible mathematical feats. But here there are two! The only explanation must be that these identical twins have nearly identical brains.

But like most identical twins, they're not *totally* identical. George, the second-born twin, is better at numbers than Charles. George is always right when he tells you the days of the week in other centuries, but Charles sometimes makes mistakes.

And if it wasn't for George, this whole story might not have come to light. George was discovered studying a perpetual calendar when he was just 6 years old.

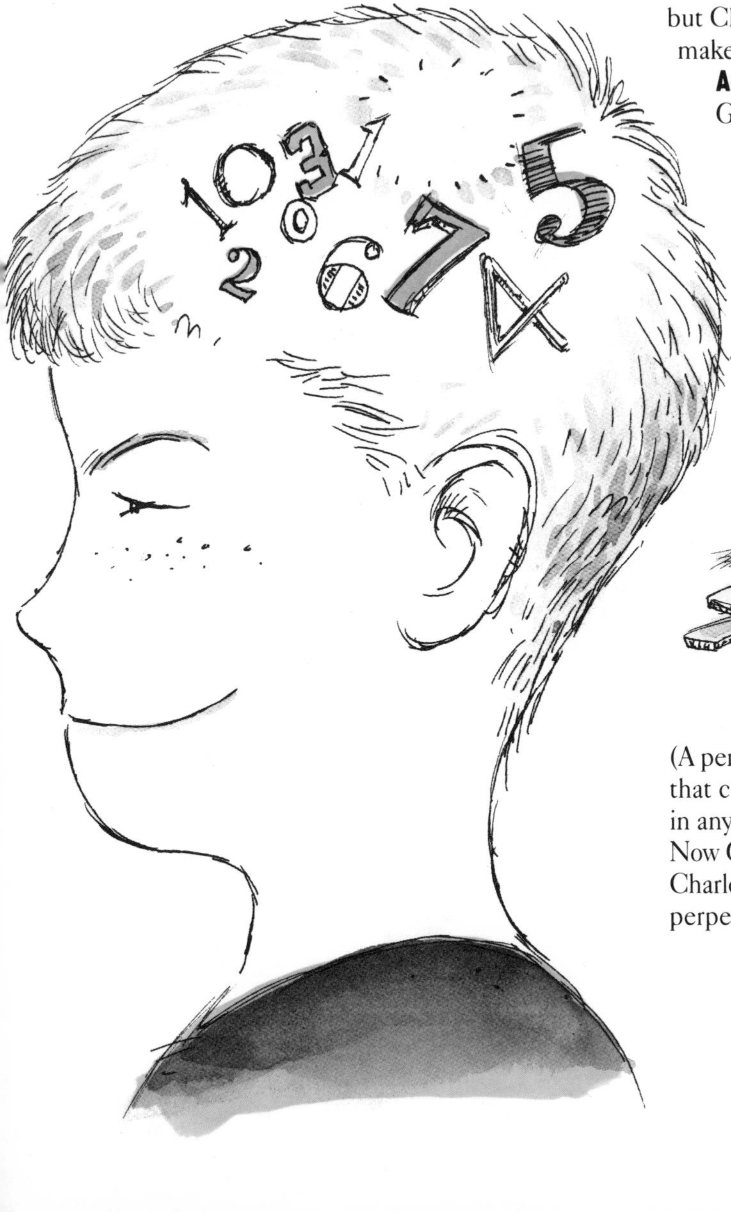

(A perpetual calendar is one that can tell you the dates in any year, past or future.) Now George and his brother Charles are living, breathing perpetual calendars.

Index